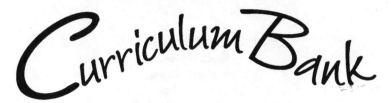

ENGLISH

Curriculum Bank

KEY STAGE TWO
SCOTTISH LEVELS C-E

SPEAKING AND LISTENING

DAVID ORME AND MOIRA ANDREW

Published by Scholastic Ltd,
Villiers House,
Clarendon Avenue,
Leamington Spa,
Warwickshire CV32 5PR
Text © David Orme and Moira Andrew
© 1997 Scholastic Ltd
34567890   890123456

AUTHORS
DAVID ORME AND MOIRA ANDREW

EDITOR
CLARE GALLAHER

ASSISTANT EDITOR
KATE PEARCE

SERIES DESIGNER
LYNNE JOESBURY

DESIGNER
CLAIRE BELCHER

ILLUSTRATIONS
PETER STEVENSON

COVER ILLUSTRATION
JONATHAN BENTLEY

INFORMATION TECHNOLOGY CONSULTANT
MARTIN BLOWS

SCOTTISH 5–14 LINKS
MARGARET SCOTT AND SUSAN GOW

Designed using Aldus Pagemaker

British Library Cataloguing-in-Publication Data
A catalogue record for this book is available from the
British Library.

ISBN 0-590-53403-3

Contents

SPEAKING AND
LISTENING

ACKNOWLEDGEMENTS

The publishers gratefully acknowledge permission to reproduce the following copyright material:

Jonathan Clowes Ltd on behalf of Northolme Ltd for adaptation of the work of Sir Arthur Conan Doyle © Northolme Ltd.

Every effort has been made to trace copyright holders for the works reproduced in this book, and the publishers apologise for any inadvertent omissions.

Introduction

Scholastic Curriculum Bank is a series for all primary teachers, providing an essential planning tool for devising comprehensive schemes of work as well as an easily accessible and varied bank of practical, classroom-tested activities with photocopiable resources.

Designed to help planning for and implementation of progression, differentiation and assessment, *Scholastic Curriculum Bank* offers a structured range of stimulating activities with clearly stated learning objectives that reflect the programmes of study, and detailed lesson plans that allow busy teachers to put ideas into practice with the minimum amount of preparation time. The photocopiable sheets that accompany many of the activities provide ways of integrating purposeful application of knowledge and skills, differentiation, assessment and record-keeping.

Opportunities for formative assessment are highlighted within the activities where appropriate, while separate summative assessment activities give guidelines for analysis and subsequent action. Ways of using information technology for different purposes and in different contexts, as a tool for communicating and handling information and as a means of investigating, are integrated into the activities where appropriate, and more explicit guidance is provided at the end of the book.

The series covers all the primary curriculum subjects, with separate books for Key Stages 1 and 2 or Scottish Levels A–B and C–E. It can be used as a flexible resource with any scheme, to fulfil National Curriculum and Scottish 5–14 requirements and to provide children with a variety of different learning experiences that will lead to effective acquisition of skills and knowledge.

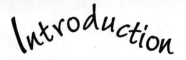
SCHOLASTIC CURRICULUM BANK ENGLISH

The *Scholastic Curriculum Bank English* books enable teachers to plan comprehensive and structured coverage of the primary English curriculum, and enable pupils to develop the required skills, knowledge and understanding through activities.

Each book contains one key stage. There are four books for Key Stage 1/Scottish levels A–B and four for Key Stage 2/Scottish levels C–E. These books reflect the English programme of study, so that there are titles on Reading, Writing, Speaking and listening and Spelling and phonics.

Bank of activities

This book provides a bank of activities which are designed to broaden children's experience of speaking and listening and enable them to develop their ability to listen effectively and to communicate clearly and accurately through speech.

Lesson plans

Detailed lesson plans, under clear headings, are given for each activity and provide material for immediate implementation in the classroom. The structure for each activity is as follows.

Activity title box

The information contained in the box at the beginning of each activity outlines the following key aspects:

▲ *Activity title and learning objective.* For each activity a clearly stated learning objective is given in bold italics. These learning objectives break down aspects of the programmes of study into manageable, hierarchical teaching and learning chunks, and their purpose is to aid planning for progression. These objectives can be easily referenced to the National Curriculum and Scottish 5–14 requirements by using the overview grids at the end of this chapter (pages 11 to 14).

▲ *Class organisation/Likely duration.* Icons ♯♯ and ⏱ signpost the suggested group sizes for each activity and the approximate amount of time required to complete it.

Previous skills/knowledge needed

Information is given here when it is necessary for the children to have acquired specific knowledge or skills prior to carrying out the activity.

Key background information

The information in this section outlines the areas of study covered by each activity and gives a general background to the particular topic or theme, outlining the basic skills that will be developed and the way in which the activity will address children's learning.

Preparation

Advice is given for those occasions when it is necessary for the teacher to prime the pupils for the activity or to prepare materials, or to set up a display or activity ahead of time.

Resources needed

All of the materials needed to carry out the activity are listed, so that the pupils or the teacher can gather them together easily before the beginning of the teaching session.

What to do

Easy-to-follow, step-by-step instructions are given for carrying out the activity, including (where appropriate) suggested questions for the teacher to ask pupils to help instigate discussion and stimulate investigation.

Suggestion(s) for extension/support

Ideas are given for ways of providing easy differentiation where activities lend themselves to this purpose. In all cases, suggestions are provided as to ways in which each activity can be modified for less able or extended for more able children.

Assessment opportunities

Where appropriate, opportunities for ongoing teacher assessment of the children's work during or after a specific activity are highlighted.

SPEAKING AND
LISTENING

Opportunities for IT

Where opportunities for IT present themselves, these are briefly outlined with reference to suitable types of program. The chart on page 158 presents specific areas of IT covered in the activities, together with more detailed support on how to apply particular types of program. Selected lesson plans serve as models for other activities by providing more comprehensive guidance on the application of IT, and these are indicated by the bold page numbers on the grid and the ⬦ icon at the start of an activity.

Display/performance ideas

Where they are relevant and innovative, display ideas are incorporated into activity plans and illustrated with examples. For many speaking and listening activities, performance is a more appropriate outcome than a display. In these cases, a range of performance activities are suggested.

Other aspects of the English PoS covered

Inevitably, as all areas of English are interrelated, activities will cover aspects of the programmes of study in other areas of the English curriculum. These links are highlighted under this heading.

Reference to photocopiable sheets

Where activities include photocopiable activity sheets, small reproductions of these are included in the lesson plans together with guidance notes for their use and, where appropriate, suggested answers.

Assessment

Assessment of speaking and listening is more subjective than that of reading or writing. Nevertheless, it is important to make a careful assessment of how each child is progressing and keep records of attainment. Each activity includes suggestions for formative assessment, and one activity in each chapter (two in the chapter 'Storytelling and performance') is designed for a more formal, summative assessment of progress. Photocopiable record sheets (indicated by the ⬦ icon) are provided for this purpose. These sheets can be used to decide on a 'best fit' level for overall attainment at Key Stage 2. Assessment activities are indicated by the ⬦ icon.

Photocopiable activity sheets

Many of the activities are accompanied by photocopiable activity sheets. For some activities, there may be more than one version; or an activity sheet may be 'generic', with a facility for the teacher to fill in the appropriate task in order to provide differentiation by task. Other sheets may be more open-ended to provide differentiation by outcome. The photocopiable activity sheets provide purposeful activities that are ideal for assessment and can be kept as records in pupils' portfolios of work.

Cross-curricular links

Cross-curricular links are identified on a simple grid which cross-references the particular areas of study in English to the programmes of study for other subjects in the curriculum, and where appropriate provides suggestions for activities (see page 160).

SPEAKING AND LISTENING

The aim of this book is to help teachers to fulfil the National Curriculum requirement that at Key Stage 2 children should 'be given opportunities to talk for a range of purposes'.

Talk is central to the work right across the curriculum, and the days of the silent classroom are long over. The early development of speaking and listening skills, unlike reading and writing, is an entirely natural process, starting in the earliest months of life. It should not be assumed, however, that higher level speaking and listening skills will simply happen. The teacher will need to plan a range of strategies to build confidence in speaking for the purposes mentioned above.

Unlike reading or writing, speaking and listening does not have a clearly set out and universally agreed pedagogical structure. Reading and writing have their genres and forms – novels, poems and information books, for example. The programme of study suggests:
▲ telling stories, both real and imagined;
▲ imaginative play and drama;
▲ reading and listening to nursery rhymes and poetry;
▲ reading aloud;
▲ exploring, developing and clarifying ideas;
▲ predicting outcomes and discussing possibilities;
▲ describing events, observations and experiences;
▲ making simple explanations of choices;
▲ giving reasons for opinions and actions.

These are, of course, not discrete areas of activity. A specific task may encompass more than one of these activities. In this book we have attempted to 'tease out' speaking and listening areas, as the chapter headings in the book will indicate. These chapter headings are, by the nature of speaking and listening, not rigid, and teachers may argue that this or that activity might just as easily fit into another chapter. Our main concern is, however, not to develop a taxonomy for speaking and listening but to provide suggestions that answer the needs of children with a wide range of interests and abilities, and to build confidence in the handling of speaking and listening. Our emphases are on speaking and listening as:
▲ a vital part of the overall learning process;
▲ an essential tool in communicating ideas, opinions, and needs;
▲ an essential social skill.

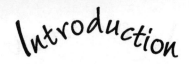

The implications of these are that, first, speaking and listening cannot be isolated from reading and writing. Speaking and listening may be, for example, a precursor to writing (although this should not be an inevitable consequence) or a follow-up to reading. Reading, writing, speaking and listening form a seamless garment.

Secondly, as with reading and writing, speaking and listening is developmental. There are skills to learn and teach.

Finally, the activities are interactive and require the collaboration of children working in groups, pairs, or as a class. Speaking and listening cannot be a solitary activity.

Core skills

Some core skills are the essential underpinning to all the work in this book. We have identified these as (1) Collaborative skills – working with a partner or group (2) Working as a member of the class (3) Effective listening, and (4) Speaking aloud.

Collaborative skills – groups

The ability to work effectively within a group is a key skill, in which the essential elements are turn-taking, willingness to listen to others, and the ability to negotiate and compromise. For some children these are all challenging. The extrovert child may be inclined to dominate the group, and unwilling to listen to or take on board the suggestions of others. The introverted child may find it difficult to contribute. Careful matching of groups can help considerably, as can the teacher or support teacher, who can act as a roving group member.

It is vital to establish a set of rules for working in groups. The suggestions below could be produced as a poster for the classroom wall as a permanent reminder.

▲ Groups should have a *chairperson*, who organises the discussion, and a *scribe*, who makes notes of what the group has said.

▲ Take turns to speak.

▲ Listen carefully to what others say.

▲ Be prepared to change your mind.

Some group work is run on the 'conch' principle, whereby only the person holding an object may speak. This can be artificial and restricts the spontaneity of the discussion. It may, however, be a useful technique in the early stages, particularly with a group of marked individuals.

Organisation of groups

Children can be organised in the following types of group:

▲ Friendship groups, with children deciding on the composition of their group.

Advantage – the children should work well together from the beginning.

Disadvantage – watch out for the 'left out' child.

▲ Mixed ability groups.

Advantage – the less able children will be supported by the others. Very often, learning difficulties relate to the mechanics of written work, and children with these difficulties are able to shine in a purely oral activity.

Disadvantage – less able children will find it challenging to undertake the scribing role, and may have to be excluded from taking a turn at this.

▲ Groups roughly based on ability.

Advantage – an able group are able to stretch themselves, while a weaker group can work with a support teacher acting as chair/scribe.

Disadvantage – less able children will miss out on the stimulus of working with more able children.

It is worth varying the size of the group, though three is a minimum and five a maximum. Where possible, the jobs of chair and scribe should be rotated.

Collaborative skills – pairs

Working with a partner is an essential part of the pattern of classroom activity. It develops co-operative skills, and demands a much higher level of involvement than group work; to quote the old cliché, 'Two heads are better than one.' Pair work can provide:

▲ mutual support, particularly when either or both of the partners is less able;

▲ an environment for problem solving through discussion;

▲ opportunities for sound boarding;

▲ opportunities for critical feedback.

It is critical that the teacher is involved at the 'pairing' stage, and has a strategy for this. Possible pairings are:

▲ Working with a 'best friend'.

Advantage – mutual trust, a good relationship.

Disadvantage – less challenging than working with an unfamiliar partner.

▲ Pairings made at random.

Advantage – this can build relationships within a class, and is a good preparation for life where it is necessary to work with many different people.

Disadvantage – the pairings may not be compatible (although even best friends can fall out!).

▲ Pairings made by matching ability levels.

Advantage – this allows able pairings to be stretched, and less able to be mutually supported.

Disadvantage – less able pairs can miss out on the stimulation provided by more able children.

▲ Pairings linking able and less able children.

Advantage – this supports the less able child, and is valuable too for the more able child as he or she will be developing special skills.

Disadvantage – this type of pairing can be frustrating for the able child if it occurs on a regular basis. However, it is important to remember that 'less able' children may in fact be 'differently able' and while an individual child may have poor writing and spelling skills he or she may have an excellent imagination.

The best advice is to have a range of strategies depending on the task involved, and to provide the stimulation of variety.

Working as a class

General class discussion and 'brainstorming' sessions are key activities. In today's pressured classroom, such discussion may seem a luxury, but it is an essential part of the learning process. The development of the skills involved in a general discussion very much depends on effective control and structuring by the teacher. A free-for-all benefits no one. To take part, each child needs to (1) develop the confidence to put forward his or her ideas, and (2) be aware of the formalities of 'class manners' such as putting a hand up, not calling out and listening attentively to others.

A class discussion or brainstorm can take place with the class sitting at their desks, tables, or sitting on the floor around the teacher. The former has the advantage of making it easier for the children to jot down ideas during the discussion, while the latter has the advantage of a more intimate, informal setting. As a rule of thumb, informal discussions are better on the floor, more formal ones at desks. For formal discussions, paper to jot down ideas enables children to continue to think of new ideas while they are waiting to offer their first one, and it ensures that they do not forget what they were going to say. It can lead to inattentive doodling; to avoid this tell the class that the paper will be collected in at the end!

The teacher should encourage less confident children by feeding them simple questions which they can answer easily. The introduction of new ideas by the teacher may be necessary to move the discussion along. The discussion should be kept short and snappy, and the views of the class summed up at the end, with particularly worthwhile contributions mentioned.

Floor seating enables the teacher to control the placing of disruptive or inattentive children, those lacking confidence or with a hearing deficit. In his or her role as chairperson, the teacher is able to draw out contributions from the less confident members of the class.

Effective listening

In encouraging attentive listening the onus is very much on the teacher to ensure that the material is appropriate to the interests of the class, and that it is presented in an interesting and effective way.

All teachers are performers, and nowhere more so than in bringing the printed word to life. The teacher needs to be aware of the key elements: timing, delivery, expression, body language and audience involvement through eye contact. A teacher may feel that to enhance these skills, it would be helpful to have a colleague sit in and appraise his or her work. It is very difficult to make judgements about yourself!

Attention span varies widely in a class, and some children will be fidgeting while others still want more. An effective performance will extend the attention span, but be aware of the fidgeters and keep the sessions short. It does no harm to leave children wanting more.

Speaking aloud – listening to children read

Listening to a child read aloud seems a straightforward task, and parents and other helpers are often drafted in for this purpose. It is an activity, however, that needs to be undertaken with care and sympathy if the objectives above are to be fulfilled.

The child can see the difficult task of reading aloud as stressful and confrontational. A poor reader is conscious of the listener 'waiting for mistakes', and this is particularly true if the listener, or listeners, are other children. It cannot be stressed enough that reading round the class from unprepared material is an inappropriate activity at any stage, and it is certainly so in the junior school.

The act of reading aloud is a multitasking exercise. The reader must instantaneously read, recognise, internalise and speak, at the same time being aware of the broad sense of the text and appropriate expression through emphasis and punctuation. In this light, is is remarkable that children manage so well! In particular, using expression and 'shaping' sentences is difficult. Less able readers will focus on a small group of two or three words at a time, often regardless of whether these include punctuation.

The task of a listener should be to encourage the reader and provide strategies for success. a listener who merely corrects errors and (metaphorically) drums fingers on the desk while the reader is struggling for the next word cannot build confidence. Indeed, there is a danger of reinforcing low self-esteem.

Less able readers and their helpers should be encouraged to *prepare* the reading of the text. Ways in which this can be done are:

▲ Ask the child to read through the piece silently first, pointing to any words he or she cannot understand or pronounce.

▲ Read the passage aloud to the child first, paying special attention to expression and appropriate punctuation.

▲ Look through the book, discussing the pictures, with the adult using words from the text. These will act as clues when the reading takes place.

While the reading is taking place, the listener can:
▲ share the reading;
▲ discuss the story in progress or the pictures, perhaps introducing vocabulary which will be encountered later.

After the reading, the opportunity can be taken to discuss the story together and to reflect on it.

Remember that fluency and comprehension do not depend on total accuracy. It is better for the child to continue reading if things are going well, rather than be pulled up over a word he or she 'thinks' is there. The listening and reading should be seen as an enjoyable shared experience, and the listener should show enjoyment of the text, reacting to its humour and commenting on its action.

These strategies can be used singly or in combination, depending on the difficulty of the passage and the reading level of the child. They can be suggested to parents/helpers/support teachers, who are involved in listening to children read, in a brief training session.

Speaking aloud – performing to an audience

For many children, public performance is an unhappy and stressful experience. Others will enjoy the opportunity to be in the spotlight. The key problems of lack of projection, lack of expression, speaking too quickly, and being unable to communicate with an audience through eye contact are problems of confidence, and cannot be sensibly tackled until confidence is improved. For this reason, a teacher standing at the back of a hall shouting 'slow down!', 'speak up!' and so on may not be helpful as it does not solve the basic problem.

The key point is that children must have a clear understanding of and empathy with the material they are speaking. The more they are encouraged to think and talk about the material they have to deliver, the more they will be able to 'get inside' it and present a convincing performance. A tempting short cut is for the teacher to provide a model by saying 'Do it this way'. This can have positive short-term results as far as the individual performance is concerned, and the child can learn something from it. It is better though to focus on approaches that encourage understanding of text. These approaches must be nurtured throughout the school career of each pupil. Inevitably, some will always be more reticent, but confidence builds with success, and success can only come through an understanding of all the elements.

Projection

Many children are naturally quietly spoken, and nervousness and lack of confidence make this worse – saying something silly is far worse if everyone can hear it! Initial confidence can be strengthened by asking children to perform in pairs, in one stroke halving the responsibility and doubling the volume. Most school halls are small enough for even a child's voice to be audible and amplification equipment brings problems of its own. Try to build up volume gradually, as confidence improves.

Timing

Children will generally read too quickly, perhaps in order to get the ordeal over and done with! A real understanding of what a poem is about will help towards a feel for pacing. Practical help can be useful, however. Time a reading of the poem by yourself, and set a target time for the child's reading, letting him or her practise with a clock which has a second-hand. This will improve the child's awareness of his or her timing. Another approach is to ask a child to imagine that he or she is a television performer who is being paid by the second; a fast performance will mean less pay!

Audience awareness

When children are reading to an audience they look at the floor, at the text in their hand, or at a position high on the back wall. Professional performers look at the audience, thus involving them in what is going on. Demonstrate this yourself, and practise with the class the technique of 'glance at text–remember–look at audience–speak'. This will help the timing as well as involving the audience.

Expression

A number of elements are at work here: body language, facial expression, intonation and stress, and appropriate pacing. Children need to learn by example; by watching the teacher, other pupils and professional performers. The work done in group performance will help, particularly with body language, as an element of choreography will be built into the performances.

Speaking and listening is sometimes spoken of as the 'Cinderella' attainment target, with reading and writing cast, presumably, as the ugly sisters. When we contemplate the proportion of our adult waking life that is spent on speaking and listening, rather than writing or reading, its importance is obvious. Speaking and listening cannot look after itself. There are skills to be taught in the early years, and that is what this book sets out to do.

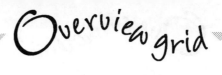

Learning objective	PoS/AO	Content	Type of activity	Page
Information handling				
To develop listening and summarising skills.	1a, c; 2b. *Listening for information: Level C.*	Class listening, then individual summarising.	Class listening; individual writing.	16
To prepare and present a short talk.	1a, b; 2a, b; 3a. *As above.*	Individual or paired note-making on a chosen topic followed by speaking.	Individual or paired work.	17
To develop the ability to listen carefully and describe.	1a, c; 2a, b. *As above.*	Careful description of route to school followed by map making.	Pair work.	18
To develop confidence in joining in a group discussion and to develop presentational skills.	1a, c; 2a, b; 3a. *Talking in groups; Conveying information: Level C.*	Research/discussion/ presentation on given topics.	Group work.	19
To develop an understanding of the concept of extracting 'main points' from a piece of information; practice in note-making.	1a; 2a, b; 3a. *Listening for information: Level C.*	Making 'zoo notices', picking out main points about animals.	Class work followed by individual note-making.	20
To gain further practice in group discussion and presentation of information using comparative language.	1a; 2a, b; 3a, b. *Talking in groups: Level C.*	Word building by comparing and discussing pictures.	Group work.	21
To develop skills of factual description.	1a, b, c; 2a, b; 3a, b. *Conveying information: Level C.*	Describing a familiar object to a 'Martian'; class writing.	Paired presentation; class listening and response.	23
To provide practice in the logical presentation of non-sequential information.	1a, b; 2a, b; 3a. *As above.*	Explaining how a game is played.	Individual or paired presentation.	24
To extend language skill by listening to and contrasting two pieces of music.	1a, c; 2a; 3a, b. *Talking about feelings and opinions: Level C.*	Listening to and discussing contrasting pieces of music.	Class listening/discussion; individual note-making/ discussion.	25
To describe a sequential activity in a logical, organised way.	1a; 2a; 3a. *Conveying information: Level C.*	Explaining the process whereby something is made.	Paired presentation to the class.	26
To encourage effective presentation of sequential information.	1a; 2b. *As above.*	Children talking about a day out.	Individual speaking to the class.	27
To develop the skill of preparing questions while listening attentively to informative speech.	1a, c; 2a, b; 3a. *Listening for information: Level D.*	Listening to a read passage, tape or video; preparing questions while listening.	Class listening/note-making.	28
To develop confidence in asking questions during and following a talk.	1a, b, c; 2a, b. *As above.*	Class listening to a guest speaker, and asking questions.	Class listening and questioning.	29
To develop concentration in listening.	1c; 2b. *As above.*	Class listening to differing versions of a passage; spotting differences.	Class listening and discussion.	30
Explaining and understanding				
To develop and improve the skill of giving clear and unambiguous instructions.	1a, b, c; 2a, b; 3a. *Conveying information: Level C.*	An individual child explaining a computer game to a group.	Small groups round a computer.	32
To give a clear account of an experiment or constructional project in technology.	1a, b; 2a, b; 3a. *As above.*	Children working in pairs explaining a science experiment or technology project.	Paired presentation to the class.	33
To improve and develop confidence in explaining skills.	1a, b; 2a, b; 3a. *As above.*	Working on 'how to get there' instructions.	Individual speaking to a partner/group/class.	34

SPEAKING AND
LISTENING

Learning objective	PoS/AO	Content	Type of activity	Page
To provide an effective explanation of how something works.	1a, b; 2a; 3a. *Conveying information: Level C.*	Individual or pairs explaining how simple, familiar devices work.	Individual/paired presentation.	35
To develop precision in giving instructions.	1a, d; 2a, b; 3a, b. *As above.*	Individuals giving instructions to a robot using a limited vocabulary.	Pair work with class as audience.	37
To develop powers of detailed description.	1a; 2a, b; 3b. *As above.*	Describing increasingly complex pictures.	Class or group activity.	38
To give instructions clearly and effectively; listening and carrying out complex instructions.	1a; 2a, b; 3a. *As above.*	Children finding their way around a map.	Class, then pair work.	39
To develop skill in careful, precise explanation and description.	1a, b, c; 2a, b. *As above: Level D.*	Taking the part of a 'witness' to a crime or other event.	Pair work, the class observing.	40
To use drama and role-play to understand complex ideas.	1a, b, d; 2a, b. *Audience awareness: Level C.*	Role-playing famous characters.	Individual presentation to the class.	42
To develop attentive listening; carrying out a mathematical process through paired talk.	1a; 2a, b; 3a. *Listening for and conveying information: Level C.*	Working on the concept of area.	Class listening, then working in pairs.	43
To develop skills of technical explanation to an audience.	1a, b; 2a. *Conveying information: Level C.*	Preparing and giving a talk on the topic of rulers.	Individual speaking to a class or group.	44

Reasoning and speculating

Learning objective	PoS/AO	Content	Type of activity	Page
To develop problem-solving skills.	1a, b, d; 2a, b; 3a. *Talking in groups: Level C.*	Drama work based on an 'agony aunt' script.	Class and group drama work.	46
To speculate with and without evidence.	1a; 2a, b. *As above.*	Looking at pictures and speculating on 'what happens next'.	Class or group discussion followed by storytelling.	47
To speculate on limited evidence through group discussion.	1a; 2a, b. *As above.*	Guessing the content of a picture from one small part.	Group discussion.	48
To use imaginative discussion to develop new uses for objects.	1a, b, d; 2a, b. *As above.*	Using imagination to suggest new uses for familiar objects.	Group discussion and presentation.	49
To speculate, based on evidence.	1a; 2a, b. *As above.*	Guessing the content of parcels from their shape or other clues.	Discussion in pairs.	50
To develop reasoning and speculating skills.	1a, c; 2a, b. *As above.*	Looking at a 'Sherlock Holmes' type situation.	Class listening, reading, discussion.	51
To make deductions from evidence.	1a; 2a, b; 3a. *Talking in groups: Level C.*	Looking at pictures of accidents and incidents, and deducing 'how they happened'.	Pair, group or class discussion.	53
To develop observational skills based on body language.	1a, d; 2a, b; 3a. *As above.*	Looking at facial expression and body language through pictures.	Class work followed by group discussion.	54
To develop reasoning skills by finding links between people and objects; attentive listening.	1a; 2a, b; 3a. *As above.*	Matching objects to owners.	Group discussion.	55
To use deduction to spot dangers in a 'safety first' picture.	1a; 2a, b; 3a. *As above.*	Looking at a 'spot the hazard' picture.	Group or pair discussion and writing.	56
To reason by asking questions.	1a; 2a, b; 3a. *As above.*	A 'guess the animal' game.	Class guessing game.	57
To use speculation in a more imaginative context.	1a; 2a, b; 3a. *As above.*	Stretching imagination by speculating on 'What if...?' or 'If only...'	Class discussion followed by pair discussion/writing.	58

SPEAKING AND LISTENING

Learning objective	PoS/AO	Content	Type of activity	Page
To develop skills of speculating by a process of elimination.	1a; 2a, b; 3a. *Talking in groups: Level C.*	A 'twenty questions' game: guessing 'what's in the box'.	Class activity followed by group work.	59
To develop group planning skills.	1a; 2a, b; 3a. *As above.*	Designing a garden for a visually impaired person.	Group work.	60
To develop reasoning and problem-solving in an amusing and imaginative way.	1a; 2a, b; 3a. *As above.*	Finding amusing solutions to unlikely crises.	Group and pair discussion and reporting back.	61
Opinion and persuasion				
To put forward points of view in a group discussion.	1a; 2a, b; 3a. *As above.*	Discussing possible contents of a time capsule.	Class, then group discussion.	64
To build confidence in using persuasive language.	1a, b, d; 2a; 3a. *As above.*	Drama work on 'persuading parents'.	Improvisation in pairs.	65
To look closely at the techniques of interviewing, and put them into practice.	1a, b, c; 2a, b; 3a. *Audience awareness: Level D.*	Role-playing an interview and discussing ways of improving technique.	Paired work followed by class discussion.	66
To develop skills in group planning and interviewing.	1a, c; 2a, b; 3a. *As above.*	Designing questionnaires and making surveys.	Group work followed by individual or pair interviewing.	67
To build confidence in discussing persuasive language and relating anecdotes.	1a, d; 2a, b. *Talking in groups: Level C.*	Discussion of 'my worst excuses'.	Class discussion, then pairs.	68
To develop confidence in persuasive speech.	1a, b; 2a; 3a. *As above: Level D.*	An animal version of the 'balloon game'.	Individual note-making: presentation to the class.	69
To develop confidence in persuasive speech.	1a, b, c, d; 2a, b. *Audience awareness: Level D.*	Individual role-playing.	Individual speaking to the class.	71
To develop confidence in dealing with feelings and emotions.	1a; 2a, b. *Talking about feelings: Level C.*	Discussion of funny or worrying times in the child's life.	Group discussion leading to writing.	72
To develop confidence in persuasive speech.	1a, d; 2a, b; 3a. *Talking in groups: Level D.*	Discussion and role-play on 'junk' phone calls.	Class discussion, then pair work.	73
To explain why a poem, a story, a piece of music or a picture is liked.	1a, b; 2a. *Talking about opinions: Level D.*	Presenting and talking about favourite poems, stories, pieces of music or pictures.	Individual speaking, formal or informal.	74
To build confidence in putting forward a point of view.	1a, b; 2a, b; 3a. *As above.*	Discussion of emotive issues; health, environment, etc.	Group discussion, then individual speaking.	75
To develop skills in collaborative discussion and planning in groups.	1a; 2a, b; 3a. *Talking in groups: Level D.*	Planning how to 'save our pond'.	Group work.	76
To develop skills to deal with persuasive language.	1a, d; 2a, b; 3a. *As above.*	Drama – complaining about faulty goods.	Paired drama work and improvisation.	78
To learn how not to be persuaded.	1a, d; 2a, b; 3a. *As above.*	Drama work on dealing with peer pressure.	Class discussion and improvisation.	79
Storytelling and performance				
To develop effective performance skills.	1a, b; 2a; 3a. *Audience awareness: Level C.*	Reading aloud a favourite poem.	Individual performance.	82
To encourage careful listening to a story.	1c; 2b. *Listening in order to respond to text: Level C.*	Teacher reading a story to the class, then following up with questions.	Class listening.	82
To build confidence in telling stories.	1a; 2a; 3a. *Talking in groups: Level C.*	Storytelling – 'true stories'.	Storytelling in groups.	84

SPEAKING AND LISTENING

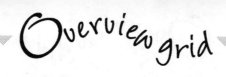
Learning objective	PoS/AO	Content	Type of activity	Page
To develop imaginative speculation and inference from limited evidence.	1a; 2a; 3a. *Talking in groups: Level C.*	Looking at pictures of shoes and speculating on the owners.	Class discussion, then group work.	85
To build confidence in storytelling.	1a, b; 2a. *As above.*	Telling stories to the whole class using notes.	Individual storytelling to the class.	86
To build confidence in telling an amusing story, using appropriate expression.	1a, b; 2a. *As above.*	Assuming a persona.	Individual storytelling.	87
To build confidence in improvising stories.	1a, b; 2a; 3a. *As above.*	Improvising stories based on places, character and object cards.	Group or class storytelling.	88
To develop drama and scripting skills.	1a, b, d; 2a; 3a. *Imaginative writing: Level D.*	Working on and extending scripts.	Groups of four.	89
To develop confidence in improvising a conversation.	1a, d; 2b; 3a. *Talking in groups: Level C.*	'Conflict' role-play.	Pair work.	90
To develop collaborative storytelling skills.	1a, d; 2a, b; 3a. *As above.*	Telling 'round robin' stories.	Groups of five or six.	91
To build confidence in working together as a group.	1a; 2a, b; 3a. *As above.*	Sequencing a comic strip.	Groups of three or four.	92
To develop the skills required to retell a well-known story clearly and accurately.	1a; 2a. *Audience awareness: Level C.*	Telling a traditional story.	Individual storytelling.	93
To develop attentive listening to a story on an audio cassette or CD.	1c; 2b. *Listening in order to respond to text: Level C.*	'Story time' followed by questions.	Class listening.	94
To develop narrative and storytelling skills by telling 'a true story'.	1a, b; 2a. *Audience awareness: Level C.*	Thinking about 'changes' in life.	Individual note-making/ storytelling.	96
Extending vocabulary				
To build adventurousness in choosing words for a piece of creative writing.	1a; 2a, b; 3a, b. *Imaginative writing: Level D.*	Class brainstorming for creative writing.	Class brainstorm followed by individual writing.	98
To build vocabulary in speech – participles.	1a; 2a, b; 3a, b. *Talking in groups: Level D.*	Looking at participles.	Group discussion/ brainstorming leading to performance.	99
To encourage more imaginative uses and more appropriate choices of adjectives.	1a; 2a, b; 3a, b. *Imaginative writing; Knowledge about language: Level D.*	Listing adjectives for use in a poem.	Class brainstorming, followed by group work.	100
To increase understanding of the function of adverbs, and to extend vocabulary.	1a, d; 2a, b; 3a, b. *Knowledge about language: Level D.*	A miming game based on adverbs.	Class performing game.	101
To increase understanding of formal and informal language.	1a, b; 2a, b; 3a, b. *Audience awareness: Level D.*	Looking at 'appropriate' language in different situations.	Class discussion/paired improvisation.	102
To gain further practice in formal and informal language.	1a, b, d; 2a, b; 3a. *As above.*	Answering the telephone.	Improvisation in pairs.	103
To build confidence in using prepositions.	1a; 2a, b; 3a, b. *Knowledge about language: Level D.*	Looking at prepositions.	Class or group work.	104
To build confidence in handling a specialist vocabulary.	1a; 2a, b; 3a, b. *Conveying information: Level D.*	Looking at subject-specific vocabulary.	Pair or group work.	106

Entries given in italics relate to the Scottish 5–14 Guidelines for English Language (Talking and Listening)

Information handling

Children often find handling information difficult. They may 'know' a subject inside out but cannot find a means of organising their presentation of it. Sequential activities, such as a description of a day out, or how to make a cake, are fairly straightforward, but when there is no obvious starting point or structure things become more difficult. It is instructive to ask children to describe their own home, and see where their description starts and whether they are able to provide an overview (I live in a three-bedroomed terraced house).

The aim of this section therefore is to develop skills of organising and presenting information, listening to information in an effective way, and responding to it appropriately. Some information is sequential, but in other cases children will need to find their own appropriate way of organising their material. Always the need to 'overview' is stressed.

Some activities require written materials to be understood and reinterpreted in an oral, 'digested' form. Other activities start with listening to information. This has to be responded to in a number of ways – note-making, discussion, questioning, interpretation. Building up an appropriate descriptive vocabulary is essential. Comparison activities, such as 'two tunes', are designed to help with this.

The speaking activities involve prepared speaking and speaking which is more 'off the cuff'. These activities are driven by speaking and listening objectives, but the organisational skills developed here act as an important way in to organising written work.

15

NOTE-MAKING

To develop listening and summarising skills.
†† *Whole class, working individually.*
🕐 *Two activities of about 20 minutes each.*

Key background information

The ability to listen to information, mentally summarise it, and write down main points in note form is a complex activity, but one that everyone needs to develop. It involves a considerable degree of 'multi-tasking', for the note-making must take place at the same time as concentrated listening. This skill will be more fully developed later in the child's school career, but the first stages should be undertaken at Key Stage 2.

Always encourage children to look for *overview statements*. These are opening sentences (or in a more complicated text, opening paragraphs) that give a broad overview of what is to come. For example, a good encyclopaedia entry starts with an overview sentence such as:

Penguins are flightless birds found in the southern hemisphere.

Picking out overview statements will improve the child's writing as well as note-making.

Preparation

Select a simple piece of text on a topic of your choice. Science, geography, history and animal topics are all suitable, though note the difference between information that has a logical sequence such as a historical event (cause, event, consequences) and a description of, say, an animal where the order of presentation of the facts is less critical. The latter is simpler to begin with.

Resources needed

An encyclopaedia or a range of information books which have short articles on a variety of topics; chalkboard; writing materials.

What to do

Read out your chosen extract to the class, perhaps a couple of times. Ask the children to say in a simple sentence what the whole passage was about. Write this on the board as an overview statement. Now ask them to put up their hands and tell you the facts they have remembered. Write these facts on the board, in abbreviated note form. Read the passage once more. Ask if any important points have been missed out, and add these to the list. (For older children, it is appropriate here to add an additional activity of talking through the best order for the facts, and rearranging them accordingly.)

Now explain to the children that they are going to do the same activity by themselves. Underline the importance of overview statements. Ensure that they have paper and pencils, then read out further text. Tell them that they can make their notes as soon as they wish, and that they will hear the extract twice so do not need to worry about missing things. After the readings, allow a few minutes for the children to add to or change their notes. Later on, the notes can be expanded back into connected prose if you wish.

Suggestion(s) for extension

Ask the children to make notes from a television or radio broadcast, or from a passage read out only once.

Suggestion(s) for support

For younger or less able children, choose a very simple passage with a limited number of main points to begin with. This activity may be done effectively in a small support group. Work may be needed on notes – abbreviations, numbering, headings and so on. Some children are inclined to get too immersed in writing correct English at the note-making stage.

Assessment opportunities

Look particularly at the ability to overview – to summarise an extract in a few words.

Opportunities for IT

Some CD-ROMs now have a spoken commentary of the printed text. Let the children use this facility to extend their note-taking skills, listening as many times as they wish and then comparing their notes with the written version on the CD-ROM. Using the computer with headphones will limit the disturbance to other children.

Display ideas

Display the original passage, and the notes made by the children, as examples of 'overviewing' to reinforce the activity.

Other aspects of the English PoS covered

Writing – 1c; 2b.

 # GIVING A TALK

To prepare and present a short talk.

†† *Individual or pairs.*

🕐 *30–45 minutes preparation; 2–3 minutes for each talk.*

Previous skills/knowledge needed
The children should have some experience in research, library and note-making skills.

Key background information
This activity is the corollary to 'Note-making' (page 16). In this activity the children, working individually or in pairs, are required to take notes from written materials or other media or from their own knowledge and experiences, and expand them into a talk lasting two or three minutes. As in 'Note-making', the emphasis is on providing a logical structure: overview, main points, conclusion. The photocopiable sheet is designed to reinforce this.

Resources needed
Reference books; one copy per child/pair of photocopiable page 108; photocopiable assessment page 109 (as required); writing materials.

What to do
Outline the task – researching a topic for an eventual talk to the class. Distribute the copies of photocopiable page 108 and explain the format of the sheet to the children. Individually or in pairs, they will now need to decide on their topic. They may well need guidance on this. They may come up with a

topic of particular interest to them, and be able to work on the talk without additional resources. (This is a good but challenging option. An encyclopaedia entry will have its own structure, but when starting from scratch children will need to build up their own.) Other children may need 'browsing time'. Be on hand to advise on suitable topics. Discourage them from tackling very broad subjects where a selection of main points will be difficult. Children interested in dinosaurs, for example, might be encouraged to tackle one species only.

Allow sufficient time for preparation. Pair work is a good option, as there is an added speaking and listening element in the discussion taking place during the preparation stage (see Introduction, page 8). Emphasise that the photocopiable sheet is for notes for the talk, and the talk itself will have to be expanded from this. If necessary, discuss the differences between making notes and copying out. Pairs will need to decide how to share out the reading of their notes in a sensible and logical way.

Suggest that the children have a 'dry run' of their talk, perhaps with a small group as an audience.

After the final talks, allow some time for questions, and perhaps feedback from the other children, on the effectiveness of the talks.

Suggestion(s) for extension
Particularly able pupils should be able to prepare talks without the aid of photocopiable page 108. However, they should be aware of its structure, which will be helpful in devising structures of their own.

Suggestion(s) for support
It might be helpful to run through a worked example with children needing support work. The dinosaur topic idea, for example, might work like this:

My talk is about: dinosaurs.
▲ Overview: Dinosaurs lived on the Earth millions of years ago. Tyrannosaurus rex was one of the biggest and most dangerous of all of them.
▲ My main points are:
1. What its name means.
2. Size, appearance.
3. What it ate.
4. How it may have behaved.
▲ My final sentence will be: Tyrannosaurus rex and all the other dinosaurs died out when...

Some children could prepare their talk in association with a support teacher or more able peer, who could act as a scribe.

Assessment opportunities
This activity is appropriate for a summative assessment of speaking. Photocopiable page 109 enables you to make and keep a record of individual attainment.

GETTING TO SCHOOL

To develop the ability to listen carefully and describe.

†† *Whole class, then pairs.*

🕐 *10–15 minutes.*

Previous skills/knowledge needed
The class may need work on left/right differentiation. If this remains a problem, you could use left/right stickers on the backs of the children's hands.

Key background information
This activity requires both careful listening and speaking: one child to give clear, sequenced directions and the other to listen carefully and interpret them as a map on paper. It is also a useful test of the children's observation skills. A good number of children are driven to school these days, rather than walking, and their journeys may cover somewhat longer distances.

Preparation
Carry out a brief survey to find out the routes children take to school. Draw a map of your own journey to school.

Resources needed
A hand-drawn map of your own route to school; a local street map; writing materials. Left/right stickers if necessary.

What to do
Introduce the activity by showing the children the map you have drawn of your own route to school, and describe the route in detail to them. Detail only the section nearest the school if your journey is a long one. Ask the children to look at the map carefully and to point out any landmarks that you have not noted. Emphasise the importance of giving clear instructions.

Put the children into pairs, pairing children that do not come to school the same way – you will know this from information gleaned in the survey.

Ask one partner to describe the route he or she takes to school. Encourage him or her to include details of trees, houses, gates, signposts, and other features seen along the way. Right and left will be important instructions. While the route is being described, the other child should draw a map of the route, including as much detail as possible. The child who is drawing may ask questions and the first child may offer help, but must not take part in the actual drawing. When the children have finished, ask the pairs to compare their maps with a local road map and see whether they can trace the route which they have drawn. How accurate were their drawings?

Suggestion(s) for extension
Ask the children to carry out a further activity which starts in the same way. However, this time the child giving the directions should not be allowed to see the map until the drawing has been completed, and the second child must not

Opportunities for IT
Let the children work in pairs, using a word processor to convert their handwritten notes into a talk. The ability to mark and move parts of the text around will help them to structure and reorder the text more easily. The children may need to be taught how to mark and move text using either the 'cut and paste' or 'drag and drop' facilities.

Performance ideas
The class will be the audience for the talks, but a wider audience will add an extra dimension.

Other aspects of the English PoS covered
Reading – 1b, c; 2c; 3a.
Writing – 1a, b, c; 2b.

Reference to photocopiable sheets
Photocopiable page 108 provides a structure for this activity. Although a little rigid, it is helpful for children working at this stage. Photocopiable page 109 is a sheet provided for the purposes of summative assessment.

SPEAKING AND LISTENING

ask any questions. This activity can be made into a game, with points being awarded, for example:

▲ correct road names – five points for each one;

▲ trees – two points; named trees (oaks, and so on) – four points;

▲ position of postbox/telephone box/bus stop – five points;

▲ perhaps ten points for an unexpected detail which is correctly picked up by the artist.

Suggestion(s) for support

A simpler version of the activity could be carried out by pairing children who come to school along the same route. Others might describe their journey to a support teacher, who can then 'prompt' with appropriate questions such as: 'Which way do you turn when you leave your house? What is the name of this road?' Help may need to be given on map drawing. For instance, you may need to indicate the correct position to start on the paper.

Assessment opportunities

Listen to the various pairs at work. Look for co-operation, and clear and unconfusing instructions. After the activity, ask each pair to write a self-assessment of how well they felt they did, and how they could have improved their final map.

Opportunities for IT

Using framework software such as *My World 2* with the 'Make a town' file, ask the children to create their own 'on-screen' maps of routes to school.

Display ideas

Make a large classroom display by putting together, in roughly the correct geographical positions, the resulting maps in such a way that they overlap. Pin a local street map beside the display for comparison.

Other aspects of the English PoS covered

Writing – 1c; 2a, b.

INFORMATION BANK

To develop confidence in joining in a group discussion: to develop presentational skills.

†† *Group work (ideally groups of three).*

🕒 *45–60 minutes, including the presentations.*

Previous skills/knowledge needed

Ensure that the children are confident in using the class and school libraries, and know how to find information on a particular topic. This activity requires a range of group work and presentation skills, and assumes competence in researching and making notes from printed sources.

Key background information

Putting children into groups of three allows for practice in working as a group, while still being small enough to ensure everyone contributes (see Introduction, 'Collaborative skills–groups', page 8). The groups will be asked to research a topic using the school/class library, then prepare a presentation based on it. Stress that they will not be allowed to read from books, or to write out and quote chunks of them.

Preparation

Ensure that you have sufficient factual information available on the topics shown on photocopiable page 110. Make one copy of photocopiable page 110, preferably on card, and cut out the individual topic cards.

Resources needed

Reference books containing short factual articles on the topics on photocopiable page 110; topic cards made from photocopiable page 110; writing materials.

What to do

Form your groups of three and give each group one of the subject cards. Ask the children to spend half an hour or so preparing a talk on the topic on the card, encouraging them to use more than one source of information.

Tell the groups that they can appoint a presenter to read out the talk. Alternatively, appoint the speaker yourself, to enable an individual assessment to be made.

During the preparation stage, be aware of any uninvolved group members and encourage them to participate, perhaps by setting them specific tasks such as a particular piece of information to find out. Finally, the notes made on the topics can be written up as a group 'mini-project'.

Suggestion(s) for extension

Extend the presentational skills by asking the group as a whole to present the information which they have prepared, either to another class or to the whole school in a topic assembly. This will require making a careful plan of 'who does what'.

Suggestion(s) for support

Less able children could form a group, with a support teacher acting as scribe. In this case, the group can consist of more than three pupils, as the support teacher's role will be to encourage contributions from each child by asking questions.

Assessment opportunities

Try to sit in on the group discussions, to assess the contributions of each child. The collaborative discussion, particularly the acceptance or rejection of material, is the key task here. Note, also, how well children approach the organisational aspect of finding the information.

Opportunities for IT

Let the children use a word processor to help them to organise and structure the text for their talk. The children may need to be taught how to mark and move text using either the 'cut and paste' or 'drag and drop' facilities.

Display ideas

Make a wall display of the groups' mini-projects which the children have written using their notes on the topics.

Other aspects of the English PoS covered

Reading – 2c, d.
Writing – 1c; 2b.

Reference to photocopiable sheet

Photocopiable page 110 lists various suggestions for talks. These should be cut out and distributed individually to the children, who must then research and prepare a presentation on that subject.

ZOO NOTICES

To develop an understanding of the concept of extracting 'main points' from a piece of information; practice in note making.

†† *Whole class, working individually.*

🕐 *45 minutes.*

Key background information

The ability to summarise or précis information into brief notes is an essential study skill. In particular, the ability to make notes directly while listening to a talk becomes increasingly important to children as their education continues. This activity builds on the work in 'Note-making' (see page 16) and deals exclusively with factual information. That activity is not, however, an essential prerequisite for tackling this one.

Resources needed

One copy per child of photocopiable page 111; writing materials. For the extension activity – reference books on animals.

What to do

First, discuss with the children what sort of information would be needed for a zoo notice which was going to be attached to an animal's cage. Point out that a description of the creature's appearance will not be necessary as there will be a picture on the notice and the animal will be visible inside the cage. Offer a selection of animals such as a lion, an ant, an eagle and a rabbit, and discuss the most important points about them. Tell the children that the information on the notices would include these key facts only.

Now read to the children the following extract on wombats (read it through twice, and slowly).

> The wombat lives in Australia and is a pouched mammal like a kangaroo. It is a nocturnal animal, and sleeps all day in underground burrows. At night, wombats come out and feed on grass and other plants. Wombats are about a metre long, with grey fur and thick, stumpy legs. They are usually shy creatures, but can attack humans if they think their babies are in danger.

Ask the children to write down, in note form, the main points for their zoo notice. Point out that the zoo notice has room for three statements only, so they must prioritise the information. When they have made their rough notes, read the passage again and allow the children to change or add information. Now ask them to produce a draft of their zoo notice for the wombat. Once this has been checked for spelling, ask the children to complete the zoo notice on to a copy of photocopiable page 111. An effective end-product would be to include headings, for example:

Country: Australia.
Diet: grass and other plants.
Type of animal: nocturnal, pouched.

You may wish to suggest this format when discussing the zoo notices, or wait and see whether this emerges naturally.

Suggestion(s) for extension
Some children may be confident enough to take on the role of the teacher. They should prepare and read out a short extract on a different animal, asking a group or the class to prepare a zoo notice for it. Mythical animals could also be included. The wombat picture and heading can be blanked off the photocopiable sheet to allow for other creatures.

Suggestion(s) for support
Making notes on a passage while it is being listened to is a difficult activity. Stress the importance of noting main points, rather than trying to write down everything. Allow children to team up with a partner. The more able partner will make the notes, then consult to see whether anything important has been missed out. See the suggestions on 'Note-making' on page 16. Another possibility would be to give the children sentences to complete while listening to the talk, for example: *The wombat is a... The wombat comes from... The wombat eats...*

Assessment opportunities
Focus on the children's abilities to listen attentively to a short talk and to listen to and carry out complex instructions.

Opportunities for IT
Final versions of the zoo notices can be presented by using a word processor, desktop publishing package or drawing package to design them. Encourage the children to experiment with different font styles and sizes to make the notices more attractive, and also to add borders of their choice. Pictures of the animals can be inserted, taken from clip-art collections or even scanned from their own line drawings.

Metropolis Wildlife Park

Wombat

Display ideas
Use the zoo notices to make an attractive display.

Other aspects of the English PoS covered
Reading – 1b.
Writing – 1c; 2b.

Reference to photocopiable sheet
Photocopiable page 111 should be used by the children when writing out their zoo notices. The picture of the wombat and the heading can be blanked out if necessary, allowing the children to write about other animals.

LOOKING AT PICTURES

To gain further practice in group discussion and presentation of information using comparative language.

†† *Groups of four or five children.*

🕐 *30–45 minutes.*

Previous skills/knowledge needed
Children will need to be familiar with the process of brainstorming (see Introduction, 'Working as a class', page 9) and of working together in groups (see Introduction, 'Collaborative skills – groups', page 8).

Key background information
This is a group brainstorming exercise. The important element is to look at comparative language, starting with simple, concrete

ideas such as bigger/smaller, thinner/fatter, and moving to more abstract ideas such as modern/old-fashioned, realistic/non realistic, lifelike/caricature, ugly/beautiful, interesting/boring.

Preparation
Choose appropriate pictures for the extension and support activities, as suggested in the sections below. Prepare a word bank of comparative words for those children needing support work.

Resources needed
Photocopiable page 112 (one copy per group); writing materials. For the extension activity – a range of pictures assembled in pairs with common elements and contrasts. For the support activity – some appropriate pictures.

What to do
Ask the children to work in groups of four or five. Give each group a copy of photocopiable page 112, and ask the groups to examine the pairs of pictures, noting their differences, and brainstorming appropriate words and phrases. (If one child in each group is the scribe, he or she could write notes in two columns, one for each picture.)

Explain that the first task is to work together on the 'spot the difference' exercise, circling the differences between the two pictures, and brainstorming and writing down suitable vocabulary to describe the differences.

The second set of pictures will require a more sophisticated vocabulary as the differences here are comparative. Look for words such as 'untidy/well cared for', 'broken down/smart' and so on.

The third set of pictures shows a contrasting style in the way the drawings of the same group of children are presented. One style uses a realistic approach, the other caricature. In their word-building the children need to focus on the way the pictures are drawn and what the pictures might tell us about the characters, as the differences here are qualitative. Encourage them to consider style, mood and so on. Conclude the activity by sharing the words the children have come up with, asking the groups to use them to 'sum up' the differences between the pictures.

Suggestion(s) for extension
Direct the main activity in the same way as described in 'What to do', but use your own pictures instead of the photocopiable sheet. Choose ones which evoke a thoughtful response. You could pair an impressionist painting with a photograph; a stylised face on a medieval painting with a modern portrait; a picture of a crowd scene in a newspaper or a magazine with a Lowry painting, or pictures in different styles but with a similar theme.

Encourage the children, individually or in groups, to find their own pairs of pictures. Ask them to brainstorm words and ideas, and then present the pictures to the class with a short talk.

Looking at pictures

Suggestion(s) for support
Many children will benefit from a word bank of comparative words, and an introductory discussion on areas to consider. These can include:
▲ differences of medium (photograph, oil painting, line drawing);
▲ differences of mood (cheerful, dreamy, exciting);
▲ qualitative differences (ugly, beautiful, well drawn, clumsy).

If necessary, use the photocopiable sheet as a whole-class exercise, building up a word bank on the board. After you have worked through the photocopiable sheet, give the children some new pictures. The children can then apply what they have learned to the pictures you have provided.

Assessment opportunities
Look for effective work as a member of a group, presentational skills, attempts to make a qualitative analysis of the pictures, and a broad and imaginative use of vocabulary.

Other aspects of the English PoS covered
Writing – 3c.

Reference to photocopiable sheet
Photocopiable page 112 is used in the activity to work through the comparison process in a structured way, moving from the concrete to the more abstract. The first set of pictures is a 'spot the difference' exercise. The second set requires use of straightforward comparative language. The third set requires a more qualitative evaluation of the two pictures, looking at matters such as style, mood and intention. After studying each pair of pictures on the photocopiable sheet, the groups present their conclusions.

DESCRIBE AN OBJECT TO A MARTIAN

To develop skills of factual description.

†† *Individual or paired presentation; class listening and response.*

🕑 *A five-minute activity that can be built up into more extended class work.*

Previous skills/knowledge needed

'Giving a talk' on page 17 may be undertaken as a useful preparatory activity. Children need to be familiar with the process of moving from the general to the specific when giving a description.

Key background information

This activity requires children to describe an object in some detail. The key skills it addresses are (1) using overviews and finding main points, and (2) developing a wide and effective vocabulary.

Preparation

Collect together a range of objects to be used in the activity (see 'Resources needed'). Where possible, the objects should have an interesting or unusual colour or shape in order to stretch the children's powers of description and not be immediately familiar to the listeners. If something like a cricket ball is used, try and find one that is old and not in perfect condition.

Resources needed

A box or a bag; a variety of objects such as cones, flowers, feathers, mineral specimens, interestingly shaped bottles, small ornaments, kitchen 'gadgets'.

What to do

Let the children, working either individually or in pairs, choose an object. When they have chosen one, tell them to place it in the box or bag. Although they can see and handle the object the audience must not be able to see it. Ask them to describe the object in as much detail as they can, but not to state what it is. For example, a football:

> This is a round object (a sphere) made of black and white patches. If it is dropped on the floor, it bounces...

The rest of the class should pretend to be Martians, who do not know what the object is or what purpose it serves. Encourage the children doing the describing to use the senses of touch and smell, as well as qualities such as weight and shape, when describing the general appearance of the object. Ask the class to try to build a picture of the object in their minds and encourage them to ask questions. Asking them to draw the object is another possibility. After the description,

allow the class to see the object and discuss how close their mind picture or drawing was to the actual object.

Guessing what the object is is incidental to the activity and it should be made clear that this is not what the activity is about. (Some objects will, of course, be easier to guess than others.) The main objective of the activity is for the speaker to assess how effective his or her description was.

Suggestion(s) for extension

Extend the activity by asking the 'Martians' to compare their mind pictures with the real object, as part of a group discussion. This is a useful activity for building a comparative vocabulary.

Suggestion(s) for support

Less confident children may be paired with a more confident partner, but this can lead to the dominant child taking over the presentation. Pairing two less confident children together can work well – they can support each other but neither will dominate. Before giving their descriptions, it would be useful for children to work through appropriate vocabulary with a support teacher.

Assessment opportunities

Listen for the overview statement (see page 16), a logical presentation of the detail of the object, breadth and appropriateness of vocabulary, and use of imagination.

Other aspects of the English PoS covered

Writing – 3c.

SPEAKING AND LISTENING

TALKING ABOUT GAMES

To provide practice in the logical presentation of non-sequential information

†† *Paired presentation to a group or class.*

🕐 *Short talks of about five minutes. These can be run together but the activity as a whole should not last more than about 30 minutes.*

Previous skills/knowledge needed

The children will need to have a thorough background knowledge of the game they choose to present.

Key background information

This activity can form a part of a topic on games. Events, or tasks such as cooking, have a natural chronological structure. This task requires children to present non-chronological information on how to play a game or sport. In this case, the presenters will have to find their own way of selecting and structuring the information. They should still seek, however, good overview sentences to begin their talk. For example: 'Football is a game for two teams of 11 players. They score goals by kicking a ball into a net.'

Or: 'Snakes and Ladders is a race game. The winner is the first person to reach the final square.'

Resources needed

Where appropriate, the speakers will need items of games equipment – chess pieces, a pack of cards, game boards, dice and so on; writing materials; OHP (optional).

What to do

Ask the children, in pairs, to prepare a short explanation of how to play a game of their choice. If necessary, demonstrate how to play short pencil and paper games, perhaps using an OHP. Tell the children that their explanations should be written down in note-form. Explain that a wide range of games is possible, in addition to pencil and paper games, such as noughts and crosses: these might include board games such as Snakes and Ladders, playground games such as hopscotch, and sports such as rounders, football and cricket. Clearly, it is most interesting if the children can think of an unusual game.

Allow 15 to 20 minutes for the preparation. See the activity 'Giving a talk' (page 17) for further information on structuring the talk and providing an overview. The photocopiable sheet for that activity (page 108) can also be used here. Stress the importance of a logical order for the children's presentations, perhaps using the formula (1) nature of the game and its purpose (2) main rules (3) outcome. Do not give a fixed time for each talk, as some games require more explanation than others, but explain that for very complex games, such as cricket, the object should be to give a general idea of the game without becoming immersed in detailed rules.

Where appropriate and possible, conclude the activity by playing the game, based entirely on the explanation. A paper and pencil game is most appropriate for this.

Suggestion(s) for extension

After the talk, allow the children to ask questions, add further information or put forward their own views on how the game is played. Alternatively, ask children to devise a new game or sport of their own.

Suggestion(s) for support

Children requiring support can be teamed up with a more able partner (but ensure that both children share the speaking task equally). A support teacher can then work with the pairs and help with the preparation stage. In particular, the support teacher can supply a list of useful words.

Assessment opportunities

Note how successful the children are at presenting a logical structure in their talks, such as an overview, the object of the game, number of players, outline of the rules, and a final comment on why the game is a good one. The questions asked by the rest of the class give a fairly good indication of how effective the talk has been in making the game clear.

Opportunities for IT

Ask the children to present a final version of the descriptions of their games, using a word processor or desktop publishing package. These descriptions could be enhanced by the addition of pictures, taken from clip-art collections or drawn using an art package.

Alternatively, let the children create a multimedia presentation using authoring software, working as a class. This could begin with a list of games so that when a child clicks with the mouse on Snakes and Ladders, for example, they are taken to a screen about the game, perhaps with a picture and even a spoken description recorded using a microphone.

Display ideas

Games and games equipment – dice, cards and so on – can be used to make an attractive display, along with the children's written descriptions of the games.

Other aspects of the English PoS covered

Writing – 1c; 2b.

TWO TUNES

To extend language skill by listening to and contrasting two pieces of music.

†† *Class listening and discussion; individual note-making and speaking.*

🕑 *One hour.*

Previous skills/knowledge needed

There should be opportunities to discuss 'incidental' music the children hear, such as music played at the beginning and end of assembly. This will build a vocabulary of words appropriate to this activity. Some knowledge of music and instruments would enhance the activity.

Key background information

The activity 'Looking at pictures' (page 21) extended the visual vocabulary. This activity extends the vocabulary of 'sound' words – 'loud', 'gentle', 'rumbling' and so on. However, words relating to moods and feelings – 'sad', 'delicate', 'cheerful' – can cover any art form.

While the emphasis here is on speaking – talking about music – the act of listening to music in a concentrated way is a valuable listening activity in itself.

For this activity the children will listen to contrasting pairs of music and find appropriate ways to describe the differences between them.

Preparation

Prepare a tape of some excerpts of music. It would be best to prepare a sequence of different pieces of music, so that one piece can follow directly after another. The extracts

should be in contrasting pairs, but the contrasts should not be too extreme. The following pieces of music, from which you could provide extracts, are suggestions only:

▲ Bach's second *Brandenburg Concerto* or Vivaldi's *Four Seasons* (lively) v Debussy's *L'Après Midi d'un Faune* (reflective);

▲ Jazz piano – Scott Joplin v classical piano – Beethoven;

▲ Stravinsky's *The Rite of Spring* (violent) v Grieg's 'Morning Mood' from *Peer Gynt* (gentle).

Resources needed

Tapes or CDs of a wide range of short, contrasting musical extracts (see 'Preparation') and equipment to play them on; chalkboard; writing materials.

What to do

Play the first pair of extracts to the class. Ask the children for words and phrases to describe each piece, and scribe them on the board. Work with the class to construct statements which contrast the two pieces of music. For example:

> The first piece was loud and cheerful with lots of drums and brass instruments. The second piece was slower and quieter, and quite dreamy.

Now play another pair of contrasting pieces. Allow the children to make notes while they listen. Once the music has finished, ask them to write their own contrasting statements about the two pieces of music.

Suggestion(s) for extension

Ask the children to bring in tapes of their own favourite music. They could use words and phrases from the main activity to describe their excerpts to the class.

Suggestion(s) for support

A small group might work with a support teacher on this task, with the support teacher scribing and prompting, suggesting a range of words for the children to choose from. Words used in the initial class brainstorming session can be left on the board or even extended to act as a word bank.

Assessment opportunities

Look for the following when assessing the contrasting statements: appropriateness, confident use of a wide vocabulary and willingness to use emotional words (dreamy, sad, angry, happy) as well as more straightforward contrasts (fast, loud).

Display ideas

The ideas suggested by the music can be used as a stimulus for painting or other artwork.

Other aspects of the English PoS covered

Writing – 1c; 2b.

SPEAKING AND LISTENING

HOW TO MAKE IT

To describe a sequential activity in a logical, organised way.

†† *Paired presentation to the class.*

🕐 *30 minutes maximum.*

Key background information

In this activity the children are asked to explain how something is made. Possibilities are:

▲ a food item, such as a cake or a pizza;

▲ a model, such as those made in technology sessions.

As this is a paired activity, some degree of initial planning is important. The activity works best if the children are allowed to decide on their own topic, rather than having one imposed on them. They will need to decide how to structure the information, then how to share the explanatory process. A possible structure might be:

▲ state objective;

▲ list 'ingredients' required, plus any tools or equipment;

▲ work through the process in a logical order;

▲ explain how the final product is to be tested/assessed.

Resources needed

Examples of instructions; chalkboard; writing materials.

What to do

Explain to the children that they are going to present their own instructions on a topic of their choice. Discuss with them examples of 'how to make it' instructions. Recipes are a good choice. Avoid instructions requiring extensive diagrams, such as those for self-assembly furniture or plastic kits, as the emphasis must be on the children's speaking and listening skills.

Bring out in your discussion a structure for their instructions and write this on the board. The list under 'Key background information' is appropriate for older children, but you may wish to simplify this for younger groups. For example, 'What are we trying to do? What will we need? How do we do it? How do we know if it has worked?'

Put the children into pairs. This can be a free choice, or you can organise the grouping on a 'mixed ability' basis (see Introduction, 'Collaborative skills – pairs', page 8). Give the children 15 to 20 minutes to decide on their 'How to make it' topic, and plan how they are going to present it to the class. The best option is to base the topic on a real 'making' activity that the two children have done together, so encourage this if possible. Insist that both children participate equally in the explanation. They will need to consider how they are going to share the presentation between them. If they are struggling for a topic, provide some suggestions.

Suggestion(s) for extension

There are many imaginative ways in which the children can consider the idea of 'how to make'. For example, still working in pairs, they might like to work out 'how to make' a perfect day, or they could pretend to be a dragon, presenting a 'how to make it' programme, using magic ingredients and spells.

Suggestion(s) for support

Some children will need to be prompted as they are speaking. You could ask questions such as 'Why did you have to do that? How long does it need stirring?'

Assessment opportunities

The key assessment to make is: could other members of the class carry out the activity after hearing the talk?

Display ideas

The talks can be presented in a comic-strip format, with a series of pictures showing the various stages of the processes.

Other aspects of the English PoS covered

Writing –1c; 2b.

A SPECIAL DAY

To encourage effective presentation of sequential information.

†† *An individual report to the class or group.*

🕐 *A short activity for a spare moment, or an open-ended session involving a number of children.*

Previous skills/knowledge needed
The activity is based on a special journey or visit made by the child, who will need this relevant experience.

Key background information.
This activity involves an individual presentation. It can take the form of an informal 'one off' to fill a spare moment, or a number of children can be asked to prepare a talk. In general, children enjoy telling others of a 'special day out' but find it difficult to structure their speaking effectively. You may wish to provide a model for this structure yourself (see 'Preparation'), and the photocopiable sheet will be useful for initial planning. It is important that the speaker should not be locked into a formula, and with confident speakers you may prefer an 'on the spot' approach, allowing the children to present their material in their own way.

Children from less affluent homes may have few family days out. Other possibilities, therefore, are school trips or sporting events, or even weekend trips to the shops.

Preparation
If appropriate, provide a model for this exercise by recounting a visit or a journey you have undertaken.

Resources needed
One copy per child of photocopiable page 113; chalkboard; writing materials.

What to do
Tell the children that they are going to give a short talk on a day out they have had, and that to make their talk interesting they will have to plan it carefully.

Ask the children who are going to give the talk to complete the questionnaire on photocopiable page 113. (Pairing is appropriate if both children have shared the experience.) Allow ten minutes for this. Ask them now to use their answers as the basis for a short talk, which should last no longer than two or three minutes. Stress that the notes on the sheet should not simply be read out. They are there to help the children with remembering aspects of their outing and should be elaborated upon during the presentation.

Suggestion(s) for extension
For more confident children, omit the stage involving the photocopiable sheet and simply ask the children to talk about their special day. Write the questions on photocopiable page 113 on the board as a prompt for the speakers.

Suggestion(s) for support
This is a difficult task for some children. They may find it easier to participate if a 'question and answer' strategy is used. Ask key questions such as 'Where did you go? What did you like about the place? What was special about the place? Did anything funny/exciting/interesting happen while you were there?'

Assessment opportunities
The accounts need to have an effective structure, starting with a broad overview, such as:

On Sunday I went with my Mum and Dad to the new wildlife park.

Listen out for an ability to expand on the most interesting parts of the narrative without becoming drawn towards irrelevant detail, an ability to include interesting or amusing anecdotes, and the inclusion of opinions, preferences and value judgements.

Opportunities for IT
Ask the children to use a word processor to write the initial notes for their talk. Once they have structured these notes properly, ask the children to develop them into an extended piece of writing.

Other aspects of the English PoS covered
Writing – 1c; 2b.

Reference to photocopiable sheet
Photocopiable page 113 is a questionnaire which the children should complete to provide a structure for their talk.

SPEAKING AND
LISTENING

WHAT I WOULD LIKE TO KNOW

To develop the skill of preparing questions while listening attentively to informative speech.

†† *Whole class; then pairs, if appropriate.*

🕐 *30 minutes.*

Key background information

One way to ensure children listen attentively is to tell them that they are going to be asked questions on the material once they have heard it. This should not happen invariably, however, as the awareness of questions to come can spoil the enjoyment of the material read. This activity reverses this familiar formula by asking the children to set the questions instead of the teacher preparing them. Two sorts of questions are required: questions the children would like the answer to, and questions for others to answer based on the passage which they have heard.

Preparation

Find and prepare an appropriate passage, perhaps taken from a reference book, a tape or video. The extract needs to be informative, but not so exhaustive as to leave no room for questions to be asked.

Resources needed

An informational passage, tape or video as described in 'Preparation'; writing materials.

What to do

Explain that you are going to read a passage to the children, or play a tape or video, and that while they are listening they should note down two questions they would like to ask about the topic. (Explain that it doesn't matter if their questions are answered later on in the talk.) Encourage the children to write their questions as simple two- or three-word notes.

Once they have heard the passage, ask them to make up one more question, based on the material in the whole passage. Do not tell them in advance that this is going to happen. Explain that this question is for their classmates, and is designed to test how well everyone was listening! Allow four or five minutes for this part of the activity and for writing out the 'What I would like to know' questions in a complete form.

After these questions have been devised, the children should have the opportunity to pose their three 'What I want to know' questions, either to the whole class or to a partner. Encourage the children to explain why they would like to know the answers to these particular questions.

Suggestion(s) for extension

Encourage more able children to research the 'What I would like to know' questions raised by the class, then present their answers in a brief talk.

Suggestion(s) for support

Devising questions and listening at the same time is a daunting task for some children. Children can be asked to remember their questions and write them down at the end, but this could prove to be even more difficult for children with short-term memory problems. Allow a support group to work with a support teacher to hear the passage again and receive help with writing down their questions.

Assessment opportunities

It is valuable to collect in the questions. The 'What I would like to know' questions are particularly interesting. Look for an ability to:

▲ ask questions that follow up *implications* raised by the passage, such as 'If that is so, why does...?'

▲ ask questions that seek further explanation, for example '*Why* does that happen?'

▲ ask unexpected and tangential questions.

Display ideas

Mount a copy of the passage on the wall, under the heading 'What we wanted to know'. Arrange the questions around the text, linking them to it with coloured thread. Leave room for any answers that are found.

Other aspects of the English PoS covered

Reading – 1b, c.
Writing – 2b.

SPEAKING AND LISTENING

OFF THE CUFF

To develop confidence in asking questions during and following a talk.

†† *Whole class.*

🕐 *30–45 minutes.*

Key background information

Children often find it difficult to ask spontaneous questions, particularly when faced with a stranger. Often visitors will ask children if they have any questions to ask, and are disappointed when there is no response. Children, reasonably enough, do not ask questions out of politeness, but only if they actually want to know the answer. However, thoughtful and appropriate questioning is an important skill to develop in children. It is important that the class is clear on the difference between a statement and a question. Very often a child will make a statement, often by relating something that has happened to them, rather than pose a question. Such statements are valuable in themselves, but may not be appropriate in the context of listening and responding to a talk.

Preparation

An appropriate speaker will need to be invited to take part in this activity and be thoroughly briefed. Possibilities are the headteacher, a colleague, a governor, a parent, a clergyman, or other visitor such as a visiting writer or police officer. Encourage your speaker to see his or her contribution as a dialogue rather than a lecture, and if they are willing ask them to prepare questions for the class.

Resources needed

A good speaker! (Ideally, the speaker should be someone other than yourself – see 'Preparation'.)

What to do

The best way for a speaker to encourage children to ask questions is to involve them in the talk by asking them questions during the talk – 'Have any of you ever been to…? Who knows what this is…?' and so on. This gets the children talking and 'breaks the ice'. Explain to the speaker that when the children want to ask a question, they will put their hand up. (This acts as a useful reminder to the class.) Encourage questioning *during* the talk – the children may have forgotten their questions by the end, which is why a request for questions then is rarely productive – but stress that hands should only go up to ask questions, not to make general contributions such as anecdotes. It is a good idea for you to put up your hand to ask a question, too.

After the speaker has left, talk with the class about what they have learned. Explain that the rules have changed and that they may now put their hands up to make statements as well as to ask questions. (See Introduction, 'Working as a class', page 9.)

Suggestion(s) for extension

Follow up the talks by allowing one or two of the more confident children to become 'speakers' themselves, perhaps talking about a hobby or particular enthusiasm. Encourage them, too, to ask questions to the class as part of their talk.

Suggestion(s) for support

Try to ensure that less confident children are near the front, where they are better able to attract the speaker's eye if they have a question. (Disruptive children, however, should be placed near you so that they can be dealt with quietly.)

Assessment opportunities

A visiting speaker gives you an opportunity to watch your class from the sidelines, assessing the children's abilities to listen with attention and respond effectively.

SPOT THE DIFFERENCE

To develop concentration in listening.

†† *Class listening and discussion*

🕐 *10 minutes.*

Key background information

When listening to an informational passage it is difficult to retain all of the detail presented in it, although the overall sweep may be fully understood. This activity provides practice in trying to hang on to detailed information. It is the written equivalent of 'spot the difference' cartoons, or the television game show idea of running a short sketch twice, changing details the second time around. Both of these seemingly trivial games are valuable means of improving memory and observation. The activity described here is amusing and fun, and yet it sharpens up listening skills.

Resources needed

The text printed in the opposite column. (You may prefer to produce your own texts based more exactly on the age or interests of your own pupils.)

Preparation

If required, prepare a text, producing one original version and another one in which changes have been made. Aim at a range of changes, from the ludicrously obvious to the subtle. It is perfectly possible to incorporate changes while reading out the passage for the second time, requiring no preparation.

What to do

Explain to the children that you are going to read them a short passage, and you will then read it again making several changes. Slowly and carefully read aloud Version 1 (below), then Version 2.

Version 1

The Moon is a satellite of the Earth. As the Earth moves round the Sun, the Moon moves round the Earth. The Earth weighs 81 times as much as the Moon. A moon visitor would only weigh one sixth as much as on Earth.

The Moon has no atmosphere, and no water. Its surface is covered with craters made when meteorites have struck its surface.

The first person to step on the Moon was the American Neil Armstrong, in 1969. The first words spoken on the Moon were 'It's one small step for a man, one giant leap for mankind.'

Version 2

The Earth is a satellite of the Moon. As the Earth moves round the corner, the Moon moves round as well. The Earth weighs eight times as much as the Moon. A moon creature would only weigh one sixtieth as much as on Earth.

The Moon has a creepy atmosphere, and no water. Its surface is covered with cracks made when meteors have struck its face.

The first person to stand on the Moon was Neil Armstrong, in 1968. The first words spoken on the Moon were 'Whoops, I've just fallen off the ladder.'

Ask the children to put up their hands when they think something has changed, but not to call out. They will need to point out not only that a change has been made but also what the original stated. At the end, point out any differences which they have missed.

Suggestion(s) for extension

The task can be made more difficult firstly by not telling the class the purpose of reading the first passage until after it has been read, thus not signalling the need for concentrated listening, or secondly by only allowing 'hands up' *after* the second passage has been read.

Suggestion(s) for support

This is a useful activity for small groups and a support teacher. The difficulty of the passage can be varied according to the ability of the group.

Assessment opportunities

A class 'hands-up' allows only a broad means of assessing individual listening skills. To make an individual assessment, the activity could be undertaken on a one-to-one basis, scoring a point for each difference noted.

SPEAKING AND
LISTENING

Explaining and understanding

The activities in this chapter take those in the previous one a stage further. Presenting information is a one-way activity, but explaining implies interaction. Explaining also implies that a process is involved. One activity asks children to imagine that they are a well-known celebrity from the past or present, for example an Egyptian pyramid builder. The children are then asked, not what a pyramid is like, but how they went about building one.

The first activity, in which children are asked to explain how a computer game works, involves far more than straightforward instruction. Explanation involves demonstrating, asking and receiving questions, prompting, seeing if the instructions have been understood and, if necessary, recasting the instructions in a different simpler form. Simply put, it is the difference between telling and teaching. Instructions are an important concept in which speaking skills are concerned with giving effective instructions, and the listening element requires that they are carried out correctly. As with handling information, it is vital that explanations move from the general to the particular, and 'overviewing' – giving a general introduction that encompasses all that is to come – is stressed in many of the activities.

The activities involve a number of different strategies: note-making, class presentations, activities involving children 'teaching' others, question and answer sessions and role-playing. This chapter is particularly relevant to work in science, maths and technology.

COMPUTER GAME

To develop and improve the skill of giving clear and unambiguous instructions.

†† *Small group or groups.*

🕐 *15–20 minutes.*

Previous skills/knowledge needed

The main speaker in the group will need knowledge of how to play a computer game.

Key background information

The explanation of a computer game involves:

▲ direct verbal instruction;

▲ demonstration;

▲ prompting;

▲ answering questions.

This activity can be carried out informally, or can be prepared in advance with a discussion of what the important aspects are of explaining a game. Any game has an object, and a hierarchy of instructions that need to be explained in an effective sequence. The speaker will act as instructor and teach the rules of the game to a group of children. One way to set this up is to allow the 'instructors' time to learn the game in another place, perhaps working on it together as a group problem-solving activity.

Preparation

Ensure the computer, or computers, are up and running. Choose a game with sufficient complexity to make the task a challenging one, but not so complex that the task becomes too extended. Load the game if the pupils are unsure how to do it themselves.

Resources needed

Computer, or computers, with a disk of an appropriate game.

What to do

Ask the child who is the 'instructor' in the group to run the game and explain it once, while playing it. When they have finished, another child should then try to play the game. The 'instructor' should not be permitted to take over, but should teach by prompting and answering questions. Other members of the group can learn from this interaction, but should not take part until it is their turn to play the game. Watch out for the correct use of 'group manners'. This can be particularly problematic at the computer keyboard, where children can often become irritated by the slowness of others to 'catch on'. Ensure also a gender balance here. Boys can sometimes regard computer games as 'their' territory.

Suggestion(s) for extension

Children who are confident in handling other computer tasks, such as word-processing or design programs, or general tasks such as loading programs or setting up printers, can be appointed as special 'consultants', or 'troubleshooters', to the class. The use of such consultants can save you a great deal of time.

Suggestion(s) for support

Often children less confident in other areas will excel at a task where computers are involved. Some children could be asked to 'teach the teacher' first. Any problems in their explanation can then be resolved at this stage.

Assessment opportunities

Listen in on the teaching sessions. Assess the children's abilities to work effectively as members of a group. Note whether instructions have been given effectively, and whether the members of the group have been able to carry out complex instructions. Look out for other children annoyed by an inadequate or impatient explanation.

Opportunities for IT

Show the children various types of instructions so that they can see the language that is used and the presentation of the instructions. Ask the children to write a set of instructions, explaining how the computer games are used. These can be produced on a word processor or typed in and designed using a desktop publishing package. Explain the advantages of using different formatting commands, using tabs or hanging indents to line up the instructions.

> 1. Double-click on the picture of the spaceship.
> 2. Select one-player game.
> 3. Select sound on or off...

The addition of pictures will help to clarify the instructions. These can be imported from clip art or scanned from the children's own line drawings.

EXPLAINING A TECHNOLOGY PROJECT

Giving a clear account of an experiment or constructional project in technology.

†† *A paired presentation to the class (or individual or group presentation).*

🕐 *The time taken will vary, but allow each pair at least 10 minutes for their presentation, plus preparation time.*

Key background information

Making a presentation is one of the most important aspects of any technology project. It not only benefits the class, it also consolidates the work done in the minds of those who carried it out.

There can be no fixed formula with which to work through the presentations, as this will depend on what the project was. The following check-list may, however, be useful. A version of it could be written up on the board or produced as a poster.

▲ What were we trying to achieve?

▲ Why did we decide to do it this way?

▲ What materials did we need?

▲ How did we go about it?

▲ What problems did we meet?

▲ How far did we achieve what we set out to do?

▲ How would we do it differently next time?

Resources needed

Apart from the materials used in the project itself, those making the presentation may need to use presentational aids such as a flip chart or OHP; chalkboard; writing materials; photocopiable assessment page 114 (as required).

What to do

The choice of the project will be determined by your technology curriculum. Appropriate tasks are building a wind-gauge, making a self-propelled vehicle and constructing a weighing machine. These sorts of tasks are particularly appropriate for pair work.

Make it clear at the beginning of the task that the final presentation will be an important part of the whole project. Encourage the pairs to keep a 'logbook' of their work, using either the check-list opposite, or a version of it. Tell the children to refer to their check-list regularly; they should not wait until the project is completed. Thus the work for the presentation will take place while the project is under way.

Stress that the presentation will still be valuable even if the project itself is a failure. Explain that scientists and engineers can learn as much from their failures as from their successes.

Give the children time to prepare any diagrams and pictures that they may wish to use. They may also like to include a demonstration of the 'end-product' in operation. Encourage older children to explore possibilities such as the use of the OHP.

The presentations should conclude with a question and answer session.

SPEAKING AND LISTENING

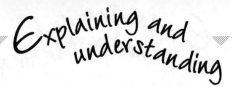

Suggestion(s) for extension

The presentations can be further polished and then presented to another class or to the school in an assembly. An interesting approach is to ask the pairs to rework their presentation for infants. This will test their ability to explain complex ideas in a very simple way.

Suggestion(s) for support

This is a challenging exercise. Support can be given with careful mixed ability pairing or by allowing, say, groups of three. Ensure that the weaker partners play a full part in the presentation.

Assessment opportunities

This activity is appropriate for summative assessment. Photocopiable page 114 enables you to record individual attainment.

Opportunities for IT

Let the children use a drawing package or desktop publishing package to help them to make overhead transparencies for their talk. Ask them to draw diagrams, if appropriate, and then add text. If their work is printed on to OHP sheets, these can either be fed through the printer or used to make photocopies. (Make sure you use the right sort or they can melt and stick to the drum of the copier.)

An alternative strategy is to use an authoring package to create a multimedia presentation in which the children can link together their pictures and writing, and even add a recorded commentary which is facilitated by a microphone attached to the computer. The presentation could take the user through each step of the design process, the final presentation being printed out for classroom display.

Display ideas

Technology projects lend themselves to display. If this is an intended outcome, make the pairs aware of it from the beginning, and involve them in the design of the display rather than doing this entirely yourself.

Other aspects of the English PoS covered

Writing – 1c; 2b.
Reading – 2c.

Reference to photocopiable sheet

Photocopiable page 114 provides a record sheet which will enable you to assess individual children's understanding.

HOW TO GET THERE

Improving and developing confidence in explaining skills.

†† *Individual speaking to the class, group, another pupil or the teacher.*

🕐 *An activity for odd moments, or can be a more open-ended class activity.*

Key background information

This is a straightforward activity, but one that can cause great confusion! In this activity children are asked to explain how to reach a particular place (their home, the town centre, a particular building such as a library) from the school. They may imagine that they are explaining this to a driver or a walker. (These will, of course, be different activities. Drivers have to contend with one-way streets and difficult junctions, for example, while pedestrians may have problems crossing busy roads.)

This activity can form part of a 'journeys' topic.

Preparation

Attach a local map of the area to a display board or chalkboard for the children to refer to.

Resources needed

A copy of a local map for the class to refer to; writing materials. For the extension activity – rail or bus timetables. For the support activity – left/right stickers; word bank.

What to do

Choose a destination. Ask the child who is the speaker to give clear and concise directions to this place using the most suitable route, describing landmarks on the way and detailing any hazards. You could ask them to include places of interest that the walker or driver may see on the way. Do not allow the rest of the class to disagree verbally during the explanation. Tell the children that, if they think the speaker has given wrong directions, they should make a note and explain why at the end. They may even be able to work out where the driver or walker has ended up!

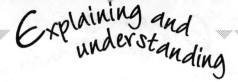

If you are not sure how well individual children know the area, ask them to decide on their own destinations, or stick to routes to school or home. (Even this may prove difficult for less observant car passengers!) Any disagreements should be solved by checking on the map.

This activity can be pointed in a more imaginative direction by asking for directions to more unusual places such as Mars, the centre of the Earth, the top of Mount Everest, the school hall via South America, or to a fantasy world. A model here could be *The Lion, the Witch and the Wardrobe* by C.S. Lewis (HarperCollins). Ask the children to think up their own unlikely route to a fantasy world. After the spoken presentations these can be developed into writing or map-making (see 'Display ideas').

Suggestion(s) for extension
This simple activity can be extended into journey planning involving the use of rail and bus timetables, and detailed map work.

Suggestion(s) for support
Some children may need support on 'handedness'. Use left and right stickers on the back of their hands. A word bank may be useful – 'dual carriageway', 'one-way street', 'zebra crossing', 'junction' and so on.

Assessment opportunities
Assess the children's abilities to give effective instructions, speak clearly to an audience and use imaginative talk spontaneously. A formal assessment can be made giving equal weight to confidence and accuracy.

Opportunities for IT
Ask the children to use a word processor or desktop publishing package to create a set of instructions for a journey. Working in small groups, let them produce a guidebook for the school, a local nature reserve or tourist attraction. These can be enhanced by the addition of maps or other illustrations, created using a drawing or specific mapping package.

If the children write a set of instructions to explain how to get from home to school or from the school to the sports centre, the word processor can be used to help them to order and sequence their instructions, adding new lines if they miss something out, or altering the position of an instruction if it has been placed incorrectly.

Display ideas
Children always enjoy drawing imaginative maps. Make a display of maps of the imaginative journeys, described in the final section of 'What to do', perhaps using traditional devices such as 'Here be dragons' and detailing other hazards on the way.

Other aspects of the English PoS covered
Writing – 1c.

HOW IT WORKS

To provide an effective explanation of 'how something works'.

†† *A class game, with children speaking individually or in pairs.*

🕑 *Five minutes for each presentation.*

Key background information
Many familiar objects, such as a pencil sharpener, are easy enough to use. Explaining how they work in precise, straightforward language is not so easy! Photocopiable page 115 has a range of pictures of simple objects, and the children are asked to explain 'how they work'.

Preparation
Copy photocopiable page 115 on to card and cut out the cards.

Resources needed
Cards made from photocopiable page 115 (alternatively, real objects can be used); chalkboard; writing materials.

What to do
Explain the object of the game and write the following structure (or a version of it) on the board to act as a guide.
▲ Name and describe the object.
▲ Explain its function.
▲ Explain how the object is operated.
▲ Explain how the object actually works.
▲ Give any tips on operation, including safety points.

Suggestion(s) for extension
Some of the objects are more difficult to describe than others. These are not necessarily the most difficult objects to use. Objects such as a stapler, belt-buckle and tin opener can be reserved for the more confident. Alternatively, bring along some particularly unusual objects.

Suggestion(s) for support
Less confident children will find it easier to describe real objects, as they will then be able to demonstrate them as well as talking about them. The children may find it helpful if you provide another model in addition to the telephone one (see 'What to do') so that they have various examples to work from.

Assessment opportunities
Look for an opening 'overview' sentence explaining the function of the object, and a logical structure to the account.

Display ideas
The more imaginative 'alien' explanations would make an amusing display. The pictures can be enlarged on the photocopier and mounted alongside written versions of the descriptions.

Emphasise to the children that highly technical explanations are not necessary. Draw the cards (made from copies of photocopiable page 115) out of a 'hat' and give one to each individual or pair. Ask the children to give an instant explanation of 'how it works', imagining that the class are, say, intelligent, English-speaking aliens who do not have such devices on their own planet. For example:

> This is called a telephone. People can use it to talk to each other anywhere in the world. You pick up the part called the receiver, then tap in the number of the person you want to talk to. The telephone uses electricity to send the message along wires. Don't talk for too long or you will get a big bill!

Allow time for a question and answer session. An alternative is for the individual (or better, pair) to imagine that *they* are aliens, who have brought the object back from a trip to Earth. They have examined the object, or picture of the object (allow discussion and preparation time for the speakers) and are now explaining to their fellow aliens what they think the object does. They may, of course, be wildly wrong! If pictures are used, they will give no idea of scale to an alien. Imagine a pencil sharpener or an egg which is imagined to be ten or 100 times bigger than its normal size. What purpose would it have? How would it work? Encourage the speakers to make these explanations of the objects as unlikely as possible.

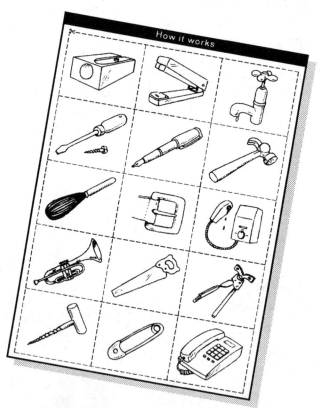

Other aspects of the English PoS covered
Writing – 1c; 2b.

Reference to photocopiable sheet
Photocopiable page 115 provides illustrations of various objects. The sheet should be photocopied on to card and the illustrations cut out and distributed to the children. Each child, or pair, then has to describe how a particular object works.

THE ROBOT GAME

To develop precision in giving instructions.

†† *Pairs; the class watching.*

🕐 *A five-minute activity or a more extended one.*

Key background information

This activity requires one child to instruct the other using a very limited range of commands. The 'robot' should be blindfolded. This makes the activity much more effective, because the robot is unaware of the job the instructor is trying to carry out. There are safety implications, however, and these should be monitored; look out for anything dangerous the robot might walk into or trip over.

Preparation

Ensure that the space you are using for this activity has been cleared of any objects which could be dangerous when the children are blindfolded.

Resources needed

Photocopiable page 116; blindfold. For the support activity – left/right stickers (optional).

What to do

Choose two children to carry out this activity. Explain that one child will be the robot and the other child will be the owner. Give out a copy of photocopiable page 116 to the new owner of the robot. Tell the children that the words on the sheet are the only words that the robot understands. Blindfold the robot, then tell the robot owner to use the photocopiable sheet to guide his or her robot to the correct location and then carry out a simple task, using the words one at a time. Possibilities are:

▲ walking through a 'maze' made of lines marked on a floor;

▲ collecting objects from one place and moving them somewhere else;

▲ picking up litter;

▲ picking up a broom and sweeping the floor.

Ask the audience to look out for robots which are 'too intelligent' and go beyond their simple instructions.

Suggestion(s) for extension

It is interesting for the children to develop their own robot language instead of using the photocopiable sheet, learning by trial and error which commands are most appropriate. An upper limit of 20 words could be imposed. This can be developed initially in groups, then experiments carried out with a human robot. The children can experiment with more complex instructions involving more than one word at a time.

Suggestion(s) for support

Work through the list of words to ensure that the children are familiar with their meanings. Most are obvious, but ensure full understanding of 'grasp', 'release', 'object'. This is a useful game for children who are not confident with left and right differentiation. If required, use left and right stickers on the back of hands. (This will, of course, not help a blindfolded robot. If a pupil wears a watch, this can help with handedness – all they need to do is remember which wrist has the watch.)

Assessment opportunities

Assess how well the 'owner' can give effective instructions, and how well the 'robot' can carry them out.

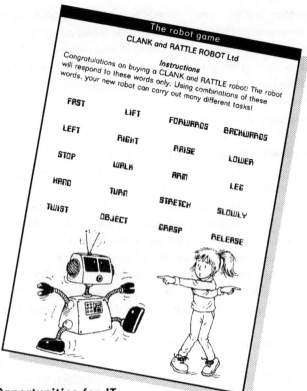

Opportunities for IT

Giving careful instructions is also a feature of control work in information technology. Give the children the opportunity to practise giving precise instructions to a Roamer to move it around an obstacle course on the classroom floor or to undertake similar activities using a screen turtle. If children are involved in control work they will need to be precise in the phrasing that they use for the instructions. For example, a set of traffic lights changing colours at the right time will show that the instructions have been successful. Computers are unforgiving in their need for accuracy and you should focus on this need when children are phrasing instructions and deciding on the correct sequence for them.

Reference to photocopiable sheet

Photocopiable page 116 provides a list of different words which should be used to instruct the robot.

DESCRIBING A PICTURE

To develop powers of detailed description.
†† *Whole class or groups.*
🕐 *20 minutes.*

Previous skills/knowledge needed

Some knowledge of scale drawing would be useful.

Key background information

Photocopiable page 117 contains a series of pictures of varying complexity. One child in the class or group has the task of describing the picture in as much detail as possible.

The rest of the class are required to reproduce the picture on the basis of what they hear. This is an exercise in logical thinking and overviewing, but using a visual rather than a written subject.

Preparation

Make sufficient copies of photocopiable page 117 and cut each sheet into four.

Resources needed

Pictures cut out from copies of photocopiable page 117; photocopiable page 118; writing materials. For the support activity – word bank.

What to do

Outline the activity to the class. Explain to the children that one person is going to describe a picture and the rest of the class are going to try to draw it from the description they hear. Stress that the descriptions need to move from the general to the particular. To begin with a detail will confuse the listeners. Give each child a copy of photocopiable page 118, which provides a nine-square grid and information which will help both speakers and listeners. (For children working in groups, an arrangement will have to be devised to conceal the picture being described from those involved in the drawing.) Tell the children that they may begin drawing as soon as the description starts. A draft version followed by a final copy is better than allowing children to use an eraser when drawing while listening to the description.

SPEAKING AND LISTENING

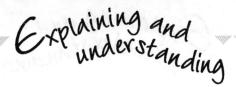
An interesting alternative for the group work option is to give the information only, cut out from copies of photocopiable page 118 to some of the groups, who should work on plain paper without a grid. It is then possible to compare and discuss the different strategies used, and how effective they have been.

Photocopiable page 117 allows for four groups, one picture per group, although it would be possible to use other pictures from your own resources.

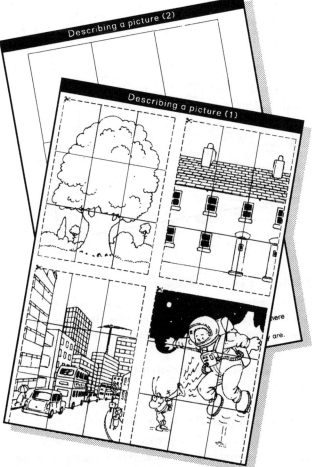

Suggestion(s) for extension

Ask children to use the skills they have learned in this exercise to describe more complex pictures, such as 'classic' paintings, including abstract pictures. The paintings can be described to someone who is blindfolded or otherwise unable to see them. The listener can then compare the 'word picture' with reality.

Suggestion(s) for support

If children are clearly struggling while drawing, allow them to ask questions about the picture, or prompt by asking questions yourself. A word bank of appropriate vocabulary might also be helpful.

Assessment opportunities

This exercise is also a valuable way of assessing visuo-spatial skills of both speakers and drawers, as well as the ability of the speaker to 'overview' and the listener to turn words into pictures.

Display ideas

The original pictures and the copies make an interesting display and talking point.

Other aspects of the English PoS covered

Writing – 3c.
Reading – 2c.

Reference to photocopiable sheets

Photocopiable page 117 provides a set of four pictures which have been drawn in a grid system. The pictures are described to the class or group, who must then attempt to reproduce them. The four pictures are graded in difficulty to allow for differentiation. This enables less able groups to tackle a less demanding task. Alternatively, the children could tackle all the pictures, starting with the easiest.

Photocopiable page 118 provides a nine-square grid to use in the activity and a list of key points to note when describing a picture.

USING A MAP

To give instructions clearly and effectively; listening and carrying out complex instructions.
†† *Class, then pair work.*
🕐 *20–30 minutes.*

Previous skills/knowledge needed

Children will require a simple knowledge of maps, and confidence in left/right handedness. If this is still a weakness, give out left/right stickers for children to stick on to the back of each hand.

Key background information

In this activity children work in pairs, guiding each other round the map on the photocopiable sheet. Working on 'maps' of the school would be an appropriate introduction to this activity, or general geography map work. The activity can be linked with 'How to get there' (page 34), which is a similar task but with a different approach. This activity develops visuo-spatial ability as well as skills in giving and receiving instructions.

Resources needed

One copy per child of photocopiable page 119; writing materials; left/right stickers if necessary. For the extension activity – local street map.

What to do

Give each child a copy of the map from photocopiable page 119. Ask the children to find a landmark of your choice, such as the hospital. Now guide them to a particular destination from the landmark. (Do not tell them what the destination is.)

SPEAKING AND
LISTENING

Use phrases such as 'Take the first turning on the left', 'Go past the Town Hall', 'Go straight across at the roundabout'. After each instruction allow the children some time to follow the direction on their maps. (Do not give them so much time that the activity becomes unchallenging.) Street names have not been included on the map, as this makes the task too easy, but sufficient landmarks are shown to aid the journey to the destination point. The children should not ask questions during the guiding process. At the end, find out which children have arrived at the correct destination and which ones have got lost on the way.

Ask the children to form pairs. (See Introduction, 'Collaborative skills – pairs', page 8.) Tell them to agree on a mutual 'starting point' which should be marked on both maps. The children should then decide, individually, on a 'destination point' and mark it on their own map without letting their partner see it. Ask them now to take it in turns to guide each other to the destination, using the same process as yourself.

Using a map

Suggestion(s) for extension
Ask the children to mark up their maps as before. This time, the instructions should be given in one go, so that the listener will have to find his or her way using memory only. Limit the children to four instructions.

The children could study a local street map of their school surroundings, and plan journeys to various places. Ask children to give detailed verbal accounts of their journey home. (See the activity 'Getting to school', page 18.)

Suggestion(s) for support
If children are struggling with this activity, work through a further sample journey with the whole class. The activity is suitable for a support group to tackle as a whole with a support teacher.

Assessment opportunities
Try to 'sit in' with the pairs, listening to how effective the instructions and responses are. The ability to locate the destination depends as much on the speaker's skill as it does the listener's comprehension.

Display ideas
The local street map used in the 'Suggestion(s) for extension' could be displayed on the wall, with the children's 'Journeys home' highlighted in different colours.

Other aspects of the English PoS covered
Reading – 2c.

Reference to photocopiable sheet
Photocopiable page 119 provides a street map of an imaginary town which is used to guide children on a sample journey, using the various features and landmarks, to a specific destination.

POLICE, QUICKLY!

To develop skill in careful, precise explanation and description.

†† *Pair work; class observation.*

🕐 *Five minutes for each pair.*

Key background information
It is said that very few people make good witnesses. This idea can be built into an interesting activity, in which the teacher asks the class to write down a 'statement' describing something which they have all recently observed – what happened in an assembly, or an incident in the playground, for instance. The versions can then be compared and used as a prelude to the main activity. This activity uses present tense narrative.

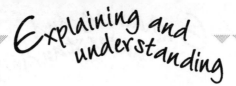

Resources needed

An object which can be used to represent a telephone; a cassette recorder if required. For the support activity – one copy per child of photocopiable page 148.

What to do

Tell the children to work in pairs. Ask them to imagine that they are looking out of their window watching a crime being committed, or an accident taking place, and that they are simultaneously able to watch the incident and ring the police. In their pairs, they will need to decide who is to be the policeman, and who is to be the observer. The observer should decide what is happening outside. It could be an accident, or an 'ongoing' crime such as a burglary at the house opposite.

Having decided on the incident, the observer should 'ring' the police to recount what is happening outside the window. The 'policeman' will have to decide what questions need to be asked before a patrol car is sent (such as the address!) and what other information would be important. All calls to the police are recorded, so to add verisimilitude a cassette recorder can be used to tape the dialogue for later playback to the class. Alternatively, each pair could take turns to improvise their dialogue for the class.

An alternative is to prepare a call to a different emergency service: fire, ambulance or coastguard. The last of these can lead to particularly dramatic dialogue. The children's dialogues can be written out in script form, as a conclusion to this activity.

Suggestion(s) for extension

The most confident children might be set the task of being a radio journalist, reporting on a crime 'as it happens'. They will not have the prompting of a policeman at the end of the line, and will have to keep talking and performing! Their radio report could include interviews with the police and witnesses.

Suggestion(s) for support

The material in the sequencing exercise on photocopiable page 148 can be used as a ready-made incident. The sequencing will, of course, need to be done first. (All children may find it easier if they plan out the incident in advance,

although extemporising can be more fun!) If appropriate, guidelines can be given on the key information that needs to be given. For a burglary this might be:
▲ a description of the burglar and any vehicle involved;
▲ clear directions as to where the incident is taking place;
▲ a clear account of the direction in which the burglar is heading after the robbery.

You may wish to discuss the key points to give for other incidents: fire, shipwreck, road accident and so on.

Assessment opportunities

Assess the children's abilities to give effective factual information, use spontaneous imaginative speech, and work effectively with a partner.

Opportunities for IT

Ask the children to use their tape-recorded conversations to make a word-processed eye-witness statement. If they play the tape recording several times, they can edit their statement on each replaying. To speed up this work, it may be useful to have another adult or keyboarder scribe the children's work.

Performance ideas

Polished tape performances can be performed to another class.

Other aspects of the English PoS covered

Writing – 1b, c.

Reference to photocopiable sheet

Photocopiable page 148, which provides pictures depicting an incident, can be used for those children requiring support work.

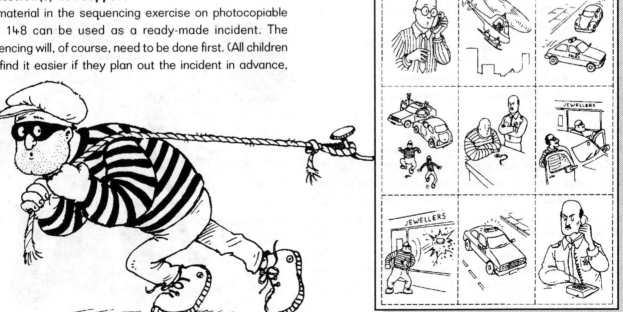

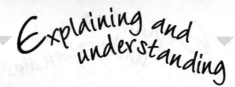

IF I WERE IN YOUR SHOES

To use drama and role-play to understand complex ideas.

†† *Class activity; individual presentations.*

🕐 *5–10 minutes for each presentation, plus preparation time.*

Previous skills/knowledge needed

For the first part of the activity, note-making skills are required, see 'Giving a talk' (page 17).

Interviewing is an activity that requires careful preparation and a great deal of 'thinking on one's feet'. Children are confident in preparing questions in advance, but find it very difficult to go further than this by asking questions that arise out of the interview itself. They will tend to ask their prepared questions and leave it at that. Talk about prepared questions and supplementary questions, perhaps by 'interviewing' one of the children yourself as a demonstration.

Key background information

This activity asks children to play the part of a well-known celebrity from the past or present. By use of a brief presentation and a question and answer session, they will try to explain something about the life or work of the celebrity. Putting themselves in the shoes of someone else can really bring the character to life. This activity presents many cross-curricular possibilities, particularly for history, science and religious education.

Resources needed

Reference books containing 'potted' biographies of famous characters; props (optional); writing materials.

What to do

Introduce the activity by explaining to the children that they are going to play the part of a famous character. Ideas for characters may arise from the work being done in class or, for a more extended activity, the children can decide independently on who they would like to be. Examples are:

▲ Neil Armstrong talking about the first landing on the Moon;

▲ James Watt describing his steam engine;

▲ Henry VIII explaining why he had so many wives;

▲ an Ancient Egyptian on how the pyramids were built;

▲ Julius Caesar on how he invaded England;

▲ Sir Francis Drake on defeating the Armada.

The children will need to research and make notes on the character of their choice, then expand them into a short presentation to the class. Allow sufficient time for this and give help if needed. Explain that the whole exercise should be done in the first person, so that the speaker really 'becomes' the character. After the presentations, the 'characters' should ask for questions from the rest of the class. These questions should ask for technical explanations from scientists, and motives from political figures.

With a sophisticated class the children can keep the identity of their chosen character secret until the actual presentation, or even ask the class to guess who they are after they have made it and before the questions begin. To add to the fun, various 'props' can be included, such as false beards or hats.

Suggestion(s) for extension

Two characters could talk to each other in role – Beethoven might talk to the latest pop star, arguing about whose music is best! A version of the balloon game, in which characters 'justify' their place in the balloon, is another possibility (see page 69).

Suggestion(s) for support

This is a challenging exercise. Some children may need careful guidance in their choice of character. Encourage these children to choose characters with a straightforward story to tell, such as those suggested in 'What to do'. Currently popular sports or pop stars are best avoided.

Assessment opportunities

Look for evidence of careful preparation and convincing, confident performances. Note, also, the quality of the questions posed by the children.

Display/performance ideas

Transcripts of the talks can be made, and displayed alongside real pictures of the historical characters, or drawings of the children in the guise of them.

The short prepared talks can be put together to make a 'Who am I?' assembly.

Other aspects of the English PoS covered

Writing – 1a, b, c; 2b.

Reading – 1b; 2c, d.

SPEAKING AND
LISTENING

TALKING ABOUT MATHS

To develop attentive listening; carrying out a mathematical process through paired talk.
†† *Whole class listening, then pairs.*
🕐 *One hour.*

Previous skills/knowledge needed
The children will need to illustrate the concept of area and the idea of a square centimetre, although if this is not clearly understood this activity will help to develop understanding.

Key background information
This activity provides an oral introduction to the simple process of finding the area of an irregular shape by colouring in and counting the centimetre squares. It can involve a simple explanation by the teacher, followed by work in pairs, or can be explained by a pupil.

This activity is suitable for younger children looking at area for the first time, and is a useful way of presenting the more difficult concept of the length × breadth formula for calculating the area of a rectangle.

Resources needed
One copy per pair of photocopiable page 120; drawing materials; chalkboard (optional).

What to do
Introduce the topic of measuring. How detailed you make this will depend on the previous knowledge of the class. Talk to the children about things that have to be measured – linear measure, weight, liquid capacity and so on – and the metric units involved. A child may think of items, such as carpets, requiring a measurement of area. If not, introduce this, as it is a concrete way of understanding the abstract concept of what area actually is, and what is meant by a square centimetre or metre.

Give each pair a copy of photocopiable page 120. Tell the children to look at the first diagram on the sheet and ask them for suggestions as to how the area inside the shape on the grid could be found, that is, how many square centimetres it has.

You will be looking for two pieces of information to emerge:
▲ The area may be found by counting up the number of squares inside the shape.
▲ Squares partly inside the shape should be counted only if more than half of the square is inside.

Tell the pairs to colour in the squares to be counted. The children will need to decide through discussion which squares have less than half inside the measured area and should not be coloured at all, as mentioned above. This may need to be demonstrated on the board.

Once this has been done, ask the pairs to count the coloured squares. Compare the results around the class.

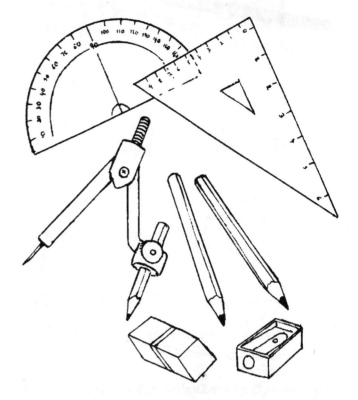

Now ask the pairs to draw their own irregular shape on the blank grid, then work out its area using the same process. Drawing round part of a hand or foot is a possibility.

Suggestion(s) for extension
Discuss with the children how a 'real' irregular area such as a pond or a flower-bed could be measured, and what equipment would be required.

Suggestion(s) for support
Children who find this activity difficult could work as a group with a support teacher. It is important to reinforce the theory: counting the squares, selecting the squares that are more than half inside the irregular area, and the meaning of a 'square centimetre'.

Assessment opportunities
This activity can be assessed as a mathematics attainment, but for this purpose the speaking and listening component is stressed, both in the class discussion and in the pair work. The children will need to discuss and decide with their partner which squares should or should not be coloured. Look out for the ability to listen to and carry out complex instructions, and the ability to make a positive contribution to class discussion.

Display ideas
The irregular shapes drawn by the children at the end of the main activity would make an informative display. Ask an able pair to write an explanation as to how they found the areas of the irregular shapes and display their writing beside the children's grids.

SPEAKING AND LISTENING

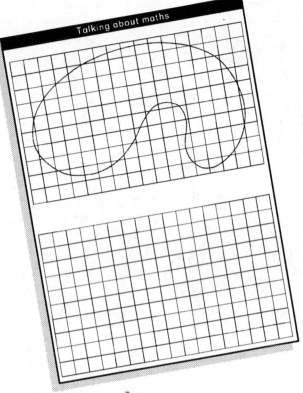

Talking about maths

Other aspects of the English PoS covered
Writing – 1c; 2b.

Reference to photocopiable sheet
Photocopiable page 120 contains two grids. The first grid contains an irregular shape and the children must try to work out its area. The second grid is blank. The children draw their own shape in this and then work out its area using the same method.

RULERS

To develop skills of technical explanation to an audience.
†† *Individual speaking to the class or group.*
🕐 *Five-minute talks (excluding preparation time).*

Previous skills/knowledge needed
The speaker will need a thorough knowledge of the subject.

Key background information
This activity requires an individual to prepare a talk on how to use a ruler, and the audience to evaluate the talk. It can form part of a class maths programme.

Resources needed
A ruler for each child (ideally, these should be identical).

What to do
Select one child, or one child per group, to prepare a short talk on the use and care of rulers, and then deliver it to the other members of the class or group. Able children should be able to manage the planning of their talk without too much guidance. It is part of the purpose of the task to decide on the main areas to talk about. Ask the listeners to then prepare an evaluation of the talk. They can be allowed to use their own initiative for this, or a structure could be provided such as:
▲ Was the description easy to understand?
▲ Was anything important missed out?
▲ Was there any way the presentation could have been improved?
This evaluation can be written, or presented verbally.

The notes below set out the key points which could be covered when giving a talk on the ruler. These are for your reference rather than for giving out to the children.

Reference notes on the ruler
Uses: measuring short distances, drawing straight lines.
Important areas to cover: scale (this should be metric only).
Any other information on the ruler: advantages of plastic transparent rulers.
Important tips: for measuring, most rulers do not start at the end but are inset in case of damage.
Note: rulers should be treated carefully, otherwise straight lines cannot be drawn.

Suggestion(s) for extension
Extend the activity to cover other more complex mathematical instruments such as compasses, protractors, measuring wheels and any other measuring equipment. Again, the children will need to decide on the main areas that they feel are most important to talk about.

Suggestion(s) for support
Less confident children can be helped with these simple headings:
▲ What does it do?
▲ How is it used?
▲ How do you look after it?
This activity could also be carried out in a different way for children needing support work. A support teacher might talk to the group after a class presentation about what they have learned, following it up with some practical measuring work, developing and reinforcing the skills talked about by the speakers.

Assessment opportunities
Look for confidence and organisational skills from the speaker, and good critical evaluations from the listeners.

Display ideas
Draw a large illustration of a ruler, and surround it with the main points which have been brought out in the presentations.

Other aspects of the English PoS covered
Writing – 1c; 2b.

Reasoning and speculating

This chapter is concerned with problem solving, and with building a chain of reasoning through informed speculation. 'What's in the parcel?' is an example of an activity that stretches reasoning skills to the point where imagination takes over. A parcel with 'fragile, handle with care', or one chained to security guards, allows us to speculate in an informed way on what might be inside. One with a label saying 'danger, do not open!' requires a more imaginative response. The idea of 'evidence' is also examined, and the difference between evidence and proof. Reasoning and speculating activities are enhanced if there is a discussion activity involved. The problem-solving activities are generally light-hearted and imaginative but even here a reasoning process is implied.

Writing always imposes a constraint on the free-wheeling imaginative process in that it does not allow understanding by making mistakes, by advancing hypotheses and testing them on others, or by modifying and improving initial ideas. Speech is an entirely fluid medium, and all these things are possible. In connection with this, the idea of 'sound-boarding' is an important one. It is often found that setting out ideas to someone else – even if they do not respond in a constructive way – is of great benefit to the speaker. The act of speaking aloud often reveals the flaws in an argument, and sometimes the solution to a problem. In theory, an empty chair would work just as effectively, but this is not true in practice!

AGONY AUNT

To develop problem-solving skills.

†† *Class and group work.*

🕐 *30 minutes for the drama work; 45 minutes for the group work.*

Previous skills/knowledge needed

The children should have experience of working in groups, scribing and reporting back.

Key background information

This activity is based on the idea of a TV or radio phone-in 'agony aunt', in which an 'expert' attempts to solve the problems of viewers and listeners. To lead into this activity a short script is provided on photocopiable page 121. This sets the tone and format. The activity is mostly light-hearted and humorous, but more serious issues are addressed in the group work. The second part of the activity is a good approach to general problem-solving in groups.

Resources needed

Something to represent a telephone (though this could be mimed); one copy each of photocopiable page 121 for the children involved in the drama session (one copy per pair for the rest of the class); chalkboard; writing materials.

What to do

Give out copies of photocopiable page 121. Select seven children to play the various characters. It is important that the part of 'Caneye' is played by a confident, articulate child. Allow a few minutes for the cast to read over the script, then ask them to perform it. The script ends abruptly, and at this point

Any problems?

INTRODUCER Welcome to *Any problems!* Here is your problem solver, Caneye Helpyoo!

CANEYE Hello everyone. Well, the phones are already ringing. My first problem comes from Mike Smith, of London. Hello Mike, what is your problem?

MIKE Hello Caneye. This is my problem. The thing is, I like it as it is! What can I do? about my untidy bedroom. My parents keep on and on

CANEYE Take your parents down to their garden shed or into their garage if they have one. They are usually a mess! Tell them that you'll tidy your bedroom when they tidy up their mess!

MIKE But the shed and garage are spotless!

CANEYE Oh dear. It looks as if you're stuck. Happy tidying, Mike! Now here's Tracy from Birmingham.

TRACY Hello, Caneye. I've got a big problem. My dog bit the postman's fingers when he pushed the letters through the door. Now he won't deliver letters any more.

CANEYE You need a small cage on the inside of your letter box to catch the letters in, and a big box of chocs for your postman! Next problem please!

GARETH Hello, I'm Gareth from Wales. I've got horrible neighbours who throw slugs and snails over my fence. They are eating my vegetables! What can I do?

CANEYE Collect up all the slugs and snails. Cook them up in a stew with the munched vegetables. Invite your neighbours round for dinner and serve up your slug and snail stew. That ought to stop them! Now, who's next?

EPPIE My name is Eppie, from Scotland. My little sister is always borrowing my T-shirts without asking. I'm getting really annoyed!

CANEYE Well, you could put a burglar alarm on your wardrobe, or itching powder in your T-shirts. If you wore all your T-shirts all the time, she wouldn't be able to get hold of them! Now we've got William on the line.

WILLIAM My problem is this. My grandmother still treats me as if I'm seven years old. Last Christmas she gave me a teddy bear!

CANEYE How old are you, William?

WILLIAM Twenty-six!

'Caneye' will have to solve William's problem. After this, ask the class to discuss Caneye's solution; perhaps they can suggest better ones! Now invite other members of the class to raise problems of their own, real or imaginary, and ask for help in solving them. Continue for three or four more problems.

Next form the class into groups of around four. Ask the members of each group to work together and decide on one particular 'problem'. Tell them that these problems should be more serious than the ones in the play. They could choose environmental issues, problems in the world today, problems in their own town. Suggest that they make a short list of problems, then choose the best. (You might be needed for help and ideas at this stage)

List the problems on the board. Now ask the groups to discuss solutions to one of the problems (not the one they chose) and then present a report on it to the rest of the class. It does not matter if more than one group tackles the same problem.

Suggestion(s) for extension

Particularly confident children might enjoy an 'any questions' activity, where they form a panel to solve problems raised by members of the 'audience' (the remainder of the class).

Suggestion(s) for support

Some groups may require the full-time support of a teacher or support teacher. If this is not possible, visit the groups regularly and give help where needed. In particular, ensure that the choice of problem is not too ambitious, perhaps by offering two or three ideas for them to choose from.

Assessment opportunities

Listen in to the groups at work to assess their work as a whole and the contribution made by individuals.

Opportunities for IT

Organise the children into groups, with each group using a word processor to write problems for another group to answer. Tell the children that their work will be saved on disk so that each problem can be retrieved for another group to write their reply, saving their text when they have finished it. If time allows, let the groups swap tasks to enable all the children to have a turn at writing and answering problems.

The saved problems and replies can be used to make a class 'agony column' in a newspaper or magazine style. A desktop publishing package is the most suitable for this activity as a page format with several columns can be set up. The text can then be imported into the desktop publishing package and worked on, with the addition of appropriate formatting. Individual groups may need to redraft their work so that all the letters and replies fit into the space available.

Performance ideas

Performances in the first part of the activity, or the panel exercise in the extension activity, can be taped and videoed.

Other aspects of the English PoS covered

Writing – 1a, b, c.
Reading – 1b.

Reference to photocopiable sheet

Photocopiable page 121 provides a drama script to be used in the first part of the activity. The children present their own ideas for solving the final 'problem'.

BEHIND THE DOOR

To speculate with and without evidence.

†† *Whole class or groups.*

🕐 *45 minutes.*

Key background information

This activity develops speculating skills, with an increasing need for imagination and lateral thinking.

Preparation

The pictures on copies of photocopiable page 122 could be cut out and given one at a time to the class or group as an alternative to them being presented with all four pictures on the sheet.

Resources needed

One copy per child or pair of photocopiable page 122. For the extension activity – 'The Green Door' in *The Complete Short Stories of H.G. Wells* (Ernest Benn Ltd).

What to do

Give each child or pair a copy of photocopiable page 122. Ensure that each child can see a copy of the sheet. Explain to the children, working as a class or in groups, that you would like them to speculate on what will happen when the character in each picture opens the door. It can be particularly effective if the photocopiable sheet is cut up, and the pictures given out one at a time (see 'Preparation'). It is important though that they work on the pictures in order, as this is a progressive activity. If the children are working in groups, ask them to produce an agreed 'report back' for the rest of the class. For class work, draw out the ideas into story form by asking leading questions. Allow the children to ask questions as well. A longer discussion time will be required for the more open-ended pictures – the third and fourth ones.

For these pictures, ask the children, working in groups, to extend their discussion and tell stories about what happens next, after the initial stage of describing what has happened when the door has been opened. Eventually, these stories could form the basis for written work (see 'Display ideas').

Suggestion(s) for extension

Older children may like to listen to the short story *The Green Door* by H.G. Wells. Children enjoy the idea of secret doors into fantasy worlds, along the lines of *The Lion, the Witch and the Wardrobe* by C.S. Lewis (HarperCollins). Encourage them to explore fantasy worlds of their own through storytelling and in formal discussion, and through drawing their own 'behind the door' pictures.

SPEAKING AND
LISTENING

Suggestion(s) for support

Children may reasonably say that they do not know what will happen when the doors are opened (particularly for the third and fourth pictures). They will need to use their imagination to come up with a range of possibilities. Help if necessary with leading questions, but do not restrict the imaginative possibilities of the pictures. If the children are working in groups, encourage them to consider a range of possibilities, then select the one which they find the most interesting and present it to the class.

Assessment opportunities

Look for really imaginative outcomes from all the pictures. Using imagination is a form of risk taking. Less confident children may shy away from this.

Opportunities for IT

Show the children how to use an authoring package to make a multimedia presentation of their ideas about what will happen when each door is opened. Working in groups, explain to the children that each child in the groups will take one of the doors and write his or her ideas about what is behind it. The information will then be linked, so that clicking on a picture of a door takes the user to the description of what lies behind it. This idea can be extended into a form of interactive adventure game.

Display ideas

Make enlarged copies of photocopiable page 122 (A3 size). Cut round three sides of the doors on each picture, so that they will open. The stories about 'what happens' can be written inside the doors, only to be revealed by opening them.

Other aspects of the English PoS covered

Writing – 1 a, b, c.
Reading – 1d.

Reference to photocopiable sheet

On photocopiable page 122 the situations depicted in each picture are progressive. In the first picture the outcome is entirely predictable. The second and third pictures require more speculation, and the final one offers no clues at all and requires a totally imaginative response.

BUILDING UP PICTURES

To speculate on limited evidence through group discussion.

†† *Groups of three or four.*

🕓 *30 minutes.*

Previous skills/knowledge needed

Groups should be familiar with the structure of group work (see Introduction 'Collaborative skills – groups', page 8).

Key background information

This activity follows the familiar game-show principle of guessing the content of a whole picture from small sections. It involves group discussion, employing reasoning and speculation, and decision making.

Preparation

Cut copies of photocopiable page 123 into individual squares and place the squares in piles, each pile containing the same section of the picture.

Resources needed

A copy of photocopiable page 123 cut up into squares; writing materials; cassette recorder (optional).

What to do

Hand out a square from one of the piles to each group (it does not matter which pile you choose first). Allow the children time for discussion about the square, and then give out a further square. It makes the activity fair if the squares are given out to each group in the same order.

Explain to the children that the object of the activity is for them to work out what the whole picture portrays, using as few squares as possible. Explain that they are attempting to do a jigsaw puzzle, without a picture to guide them! The first group to work this out is the winner. Ask them not to shout out the answer but to write it down, for your inspection. This will mean that other groups will be able to continue.

When all the groups have solved the puzzle, talk with them about which clues in the squares helped them to work out what the picture was.

Suggestion(s) for extension

The picture on the photocopiable sheet is relatively straightforward. Extend the activity by using more complex pictures, cut up into smaller pieces, perhaps taken from magazines and newspaper supplements.

Suggestion(s) for support

An easier version of the game is to use a grid sheet. As the squares are handed out, you can announce which grid square they should be placed in – top right, bottom centre, middle and so on. The children can prepare for this activity by marking up an A4 sheet themselves with an appropriate-sized grid. (They will not know, however, which way up their picture squares should go!)

Assessment opportunities

The important element in this activity is the reasoning and speculation based on evidence that comes from group discussion. Try and listen to each group, or even ask them to work with a cassette recorder.

Display ideas

Ask the class, perhaps working in pairs, to select one section of a picture from an old copy of a colour magazine. They should then cut it out and attach it to a display board. People looking at the display will have to try and guess what the whole picture portrays from the small section which is visible. The remainder of the picture can be included (see below) in such a way that after the guess the whole picture can be remade.

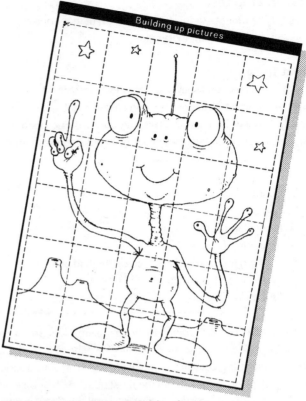

Building up pictures

Reference to photocopiable sheet

Photocopiable page 123 contains a picture drawn in individual sections. The sections should be cut out and distributed to the children who must try to guess, using as few sections as possible, what the picture depicts.

20 THINGS TO DO WITH A MYSTERY OBJECT

To use imaginative discussion to develop new uses for objects.

†† *Group discussion and presentation.*

⏱ *15 minutes.*

Key background information

In this activity each group is given either a familiar or an unlikely object and is asked to come up with as many uses as they can for it. The more wildly imaginative the better! The activity develops imagination and lateral thinking by asking children to look at things from different perspectives. Generally children will attempt to outdo each other by thinking up increasingly unusual ideas.

Preparation

Collect together a range of objects to use in the activity. Possibilities are general classroom paraphernalia, kitchen gadgets, empty packaging, pine cones, spider plants, tools and toys. The less complex the object, the more possible uses there are for it.

Resources needed

A variety of objects (see 'Preparation') – at least one object for each group; writing materials.

What to do

Select one object and show it to the whole class. Hold it up and ask the children to think of how many different things, sensible or silly, it could be used for. Reading the following poem will suggest just how far they may allow their imaginations to travel.

> I'm just a cracked saucer,
> But in my dreams
> I could be
> A spaceship for tiny aliens,
> A circus ring for ants,
> Something for a seal to balance on the end of its nose,
> A hub-cap for a china car,
> A dangerous frisbee!

Now give out an object to each group. Ask them to brainstorm ideas for its uses, appointing a scribe to write them down. Making the activity competitive will give an added spur; which group can come up with the most uses for their object?

The activity can be extended as a 'round the class' game, with children having to think up more and more extravagant and unlikely ideas.

The activity can lead to poetry writing, using the pattern in the saucer poem:

> I'm just a _____,
> But in my dreams
> I could be
> A...

Suggestion(s) for extension

Set targets and time limits for children requiring extension work. A more difficult exercise is to ask groups to choose an object in secret, then write the list of uses for it in such a way that it forms a riddle which the rest of the class will have to solve. The saucer poem works in this way if the first line is omitted.

Suggestion(s) for support

Some children will find it difficult to make the sort of imaginative leaps suggested in the poem. Support them by offering hints such as 'Could you use this object in a zoo/in space/in the garden for something?' Suggest that they are looking at the object 'through the wrong end of a telescope' and that in reality it is much bigger or smaller. Thus the saucer can turn into a flying saucer.

Assessment opportunities

Listen in on the groups to observe who is taking the lead in thinking of new ideas. Often, children who are less able in practical writing skills can flourish in this type of activity.

Opportunities for IT

Let the children use an authoring package to write an interactive presentation about the objects, using a riddle format. The riddle could be written on one screen page with a number of suggested answers either on the same page or on a linked page (the latter would extend the children's memory skills as well). By clicking on an answer the child is either given a reward (sound or animated picture), taken to the next riddle or returned to the original riddle for another go. Part of this exercise could involve making up realistic alternatives to the correct answer... the art of a good multiple-choice test!

Display ideas

If children write poems, these can be displayed alongside the objects or pictures of the objects that inspired them. The poems made into riddles, as suggested in the extension activity, could be displayed. Readers must try to guess what the 'real' object is. They can confirm the guess by lifting up a flap which reveals the object.

Other aspects of the English PoS covered

Writing – 1a, b, c; 2b; 3c.

WHAT'S IN THE PARCEL?

To speculate, based on evidence.

⋔ *Pairs.*

🕐 *20–30 minutes.*

Key background information

This activity further extends the ability of children to think imaginatively. The activity moves from straightforward deduction to more complex speculation.

Resources needed

One copy per pair of photocopiable page 124; writing materials; photocopiable assessment page 125 (as required). For the support activity – one copy per pair of a sheet of words or drawings which relate to the parcels on the photocopiable sheet.

What to do

Give out the copies of photocopiable page 124, which shows a range of parcels. Most of the packages have clues to their contents; some are easier than others. Ask the children, in pairs, to discuss what might be in each parcel, and then to write their ideas in the space below each picture. The pictures are not drawn to a particular scale, so the children can imagine the parcels are any size they wish.

When all the children have finished, ask each pair about their conclusions and how they reached them. The following questions can be asked:

▲ How did you decide?
▲ Did you both agree?
▲ Did you think of any other things that might have been in the parcels?

If other pairs have reached different conclusions about what is in each parcel, ask them to explain the reasons for their decisions.

Suggestion(s) for extension

Ask the children, working in pairs, to discuss what would be appropriate for the design of a box for something unlikely, such as an elephant, the world's most deadly poison, the sun, a horrible day, happiness, war, winter... They should then present their idea to the class, explaining their design.

Suggestion(s) for support

Make sure that all the children are able to understand the labels on the parcels. You may need to explain words such as 'fragile'. A simpler activity is to give out either a sheet of words or pictures of the items in the parcels. The pairs can then work on these words/pictures and the photocopiable sheet as a matching exercise.

Assessment opportunities

Listen in on the pairs to assess the quality of reasoning, negotiating and use of imagination. This is an appropriate activity for summative assessment and a photocopiable record sheet is provided on page 125.

Display ideas

The boxes designed in the extension activity would make attractive displays. The parcels and boxes can be drawn with lift-up flaps, allowing them to be 'opened' to reveal writing underneath explaining what is inside them.

The parcels on the photocopiable sheet can be enlarged on the photocopier and used in the same way.

Other aspects of the English PoS covered

Writing – 1a, b, c; 2b; 3c.

Reference to photocopiable sheets

Photocopiable page 124 shows a number of different parcels. In pairs, the children should discuss each box and decide on its possible contents. Photocopiable page 125 is a sheet provided for the purposes of summative assessment.

BEING A DETECTIVE

To develop reasoning and speculating skills.
†† *Individual class listening, reading and discussion.*
🕐 *30 minutes.*

Key background information

In this activity photocopiable pages 126 and 127 contain a spoof extract from a Sherlock Holmes-type story, in which the detective makes various deductions after examining an object. This activity points the way to reasoning through discussion. In the Holmes stories, the Dr Watson character is used as a 'sounding-board' to allow the detective to articulate his theories. We are all familiar with the experience of coming to an understanding by 'talking it through', even if the person listening makes no spoken contribution.

Resources needed

One copy per child of photocopiable pages 126 and 127; chalkboard; writing materials. For the extension activity – a Sherlock Holmes story; a range of topics.

What to do

Introduce the topic by talking about detectives, and how they work. Children may have seen *Sherlock Holmes* on television, or have read one of the Conan Doyle stories. The key words to explain are 'evidence', 'clue' and 'deduction'. Note that a clue may or may not be evidence.

Read out the text on photocopiable page 126 to the children. Then give each child a copy of this photocopiable sheet for silent reading and as a memory refresher. The picture of the briefcase will provide clues about the appearance of the case.

Initiate a class discussion on how the detective made his deductions. Take each one in turn and list the possible clues which Jones might have used to come to his conclusions. Note them on the board.

Finally, give out copies of photocopiable page 127. Allow the children to read this silently, or read it aloud if appropriate. Discuss how far the guesses made by the children match the information on the sheet.

Suggestion(s) for extension

Read a Sherlock Holmes story to the class. *The Adventure of the Blue Carbuncle* is a good choice, as this contains similar examples of deduction. Be aware of the period feel to the text, and the allusions to things (such as gas lighting) with which the class will not be familiar.

Encourage the children, perhaps working in groups, to try to be detectives by looking at a range of objects and attempting to make deductions: What was the object for? What sort of person owned it? What caused the marks/damage on the object? Discuss the process of 'sound-boarding' (see 'Key background information') and encourage this in the group work.

Suggestion(s) for support

Some children may need help with reading the text. If you feel it is appropriate, give out copies of photocopiable page 126 before reading it aloud, allowing the children to read along with it. You may need to explain some of the vocabulary, although 'evidence', 'deduction', and 'clue' should have been discussed already. After discussion, photocopiable page 127 may then be given out, before being read aloud to the children.

Assessment opportunities

Look out for imaginative speculation in the class discussion. In the extension activity group work, note those children using 'sound-boarding' to develop their ideas.

Display/performance ideas

Any objects used for making deductions can be displayed, along with written clues and deductions. The scene depicted on the photocopiable sheets can be turned into a script by highlighting the dialogue of Jones or Wotnot in different colours. Children could then perform it as a short play.

Other aspects of the English PoS covered

Reading – 1c; 2b, c.

Reference to photocopiable sheets

Photocopiable pages 126 and 127 feature a short 'Sherlock Holmes' parody. The second sheet should not be given out until the problems in the first sheet have been discussed fully. The sheets can also be used for scripted drama work in pairs (see 'Display/performance ideas').

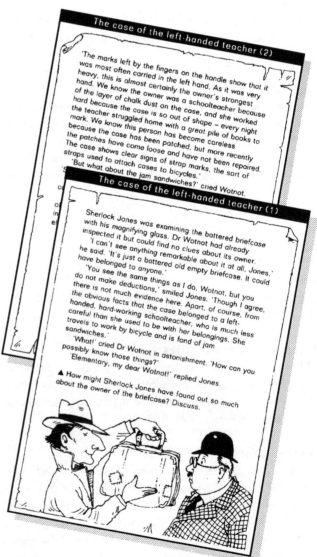

The case of the left-handed teacher (2)

'The marks left by the fingers on the handle show that it was most often carried in the left hand. As it was very heavy, this is almost certainly the owner's strongest hand. We know the owner was a schoolteacher because of the layer of chalk dust on the case, and she worked hard because the case is so out of shape – every night the teacher struggled home with a great pile of books to mark. We know this person has become careless because the case has been patched, but more recently the patches have come loose and have not been repaired. The case shows clear signs of strap marks, the sort of straps used to attach cases to bicycles.'

'But what about the jam sandwiches?' cried Wotnot.

The case of the left-handed teacher (1)

Sherlock Jones was examining the battered briefcase with his magnifying glass. Dr Wotnot had already inspected it but could find no clues about its owner.

'I can't see anything remarkable about it at all, Jones,' he said. 'It's just a battered old empty briefcase. It could have belonged to anyone.'

'You see the same things as I do, Wotnot, but you do not make deductions,' smiled Jones. 'Though I agree, there is not much evidence here. Apart, of course, from the obvious facts that the case belonged to a left-handed, hard-working schoolteacher, who is much less careful than she used to be with her belongings. She travels to work by bicycle and is fond of jam sandwiches.'

'What!' cried Dr Wotnot in astonishment. 'How can you possibly know those things?'

'Elementary, my dear Wotnot!' replied Jones.

▲ How might Sherlock Jones have found out so much about the owner of the briefcase? Discuss.

SPEAKING AND LISTENING

HOW DID IT HAPPEN?

To make deductions from evidence.

†† *Pair, group or class discussion.*

🕐 *30 minutes.*

Key background information

In this activity the children are shown pictures on a photocopiable sheet which depict a series of situations, and are asked to deduce 'how it happened'. The pictures are graded, from very simple cause-and-effect situations, to a picture which is totally speculative. The activity requires children to construct a chain of reasoning and test it. Pair or group work allows for 'sound-boarding' when discussing more speculative pictures.

Resources needed

One copy per child or group of photocopiable page 128; newspaper articles/photographs; writing materials.

What to do

Introduce the topic of 'how it happened' with real examples: incidents at school, in the locality or currently in the news. If available, bring in appropriate newspaper clippings. Look particularly for disasters caused by a series of events.

Decide whether the children are to work in pairs, groups or as a class. One option is to work on the first one or two pictures as a class, then leave the rest for pair or group work.

Ask the children to study the pictures and discuss 'how it happened'. Point out that the pictures have 'clues', but the responses will have to be imaginative ones, some more so than others. Could any of the pictures have more than one explanation? Explain that the more imaginative the stories are the better. Group and pair discussion should be followed by a report back on 'how it happened'.

Suggestion(s) for extension

The second picture can be used as the stimulus for an activity which involves making verbal statements, with children assuming the role of one of the witnesses in the picture. Work on the last two pictures can lead to storytelling and story writing. Use the following events for some 'off-the-cuff' storytelling about 'how it happened':

▲ a tree fallen by the side of the road;

▲ a person covered in mud;

▲ a large hole in the classroom floor;

▲ a dustbin on its side, with rubbish everywhere;

▲ a dog with a torn piece of clothing in its mouth.

Use newspaper photographs or articles which involve more complex situations to give the children more challenging work. If using newspaper articles, do not reveal how the incidents happened, but allow the children to speculate through group discussion. If copies of the articles are made, groups could come up with a range of ideas about 'how it happened'. Conclude the activity by reading the complete account.

Suggestion(s) for support

Some children may find it difficult to speculate, on the last two pictures in particular, and may need help or prompting with questions such as, 'Was it an accident? Who was in the wrong?'

Assessment opportunities

Look particularly for the ability to speculate, and to build up a chain of events leading to the situations in the pictures.

Display/performance ideas

Make a 'How did it happen?' display. Enlarge the pictures on photocopiable page 128 and surround them with the writing which has been carried out in the extension activity.

A 'Guess what happened to me?' session in which children wear fake bandages and so on can make an amusing performance. They will need to plan a short monologue giving a humorous account of what happened to them.

Other aspects of the English PoS covered

Writing – 1a, b, c; 2b.

Reading – 1b.

Reference to photocopiable sheet

Photocopiable page 128 contains four pictures depicting various incidents. The children are asked to study the pictures and discuss how the incidents may have occurred.

SPEAKING AND LISTENING

WHAT ARE THEY SAYING?

To develop observation skills based on body language.
†† *Class work, followed by pair or group discussion.*
🕐 *30 minutes.*

Key background information
The recognition of body language and facial expression is a vital adjunct to effective listening. Children soon learn to recognise 'moods' in adults and friends from the way that they behave, and learn to imitate them. The photocopiable sheet used in this activity stimulates discussion which will initiate work in this area.

Resources needed
One copy per pair or group of photocopiable page 129; a range of photographs of people (from magazines, colour supplements and so on) which convey a variety of feelings and emotions; writing materials. For the extension activity – television and video recorder; set of word cards.

What to do
Build up a class vocabulary of emotions and feelings by brainstorming key words, and making a wall chart of them. Discuss appropriate colours in which the words may be written, for example red for 'angry', blue for 'sad', and use these in the wall chart.
Include:

angry	sad	bored
embarrassed	surprised	
puzzled	amused	sulky
happy	sleepy	
disgusted	naughty	snooty

Show how a few lines on a picture of a face can portray feeling. Demonstrate how people use their arms and hands to express feelings: hands spread out and shoulders lifted to show 'I haven't got a clue'; arms akimbo to show exasperation; folded arms to show sternness; a raised fist to show anger. If possible, display pictures of people (include bodies as well as faces), and ask the children to guess the feelings which are depicted. Suggest they try some of the expressions for themselves.

Give out copies of photocopiable page 129 to the children working in pairs or groups. Explain that for each picture they should decide what the characters might be saying. This should be written down on a separate piece of paper, set out properly using speech marks. (One person from the group should take the part of the scribe.) Explain that a great deal of imagination is required in the exercise, and that there are no 'right' answers.

Body language is a good topic for drama work based on mime. Extend the ideas on the photocopiable sheet by asking individual children to be 'living' pictures, adopting an appropriate pose and expression for a situation of their choice: winning a competition, falling into a patch of stinging nettles, seeing someone slip on a banana skin, finding (and eating) a slug in a salad, and so on. The other children can then attempt to guess the situation.

Suggestion(s) for extension
Let the children watch a video with the sound turned down. A soap opera is suitable for this. How far is it possible to guess what is going on? Alternatively, make a set of cards, each featuring one of the feelings or emotions listed in the main activity. In pairs, give the children one card at a time and ask them to adopt the pose suggested on it. The other partner should attempt to guess the word on the card.

Suggestion(s) for support
Some children may need to work with a support teacher, who could scribe their ideas. Alternatively, treat the activity entirely as an oral exercise, with the group simply discussing the pictures with a helper and each other.

Assessment opportunities
Listen in to the groups at work; note, in particular, individual children's abilities to produce imaginative speech.

Opportunities for IT
Ask a child in each pair or group to use a word processor to write out dialogue which is appropriate to the pictures. The writing task is quite short, so the children could use a drawing package to draw speech bubbles or import a speech bubble from clip art, then format text to fit inside the speech bubbles. Print these out and display them around the original picture.

Display/performance ideas

Pictures drawn of people in various moods could make an attractive display. Mimes in which one or two children tell a short story entirely in mime can be developed into a performance for presentation to an audience. Examples might be opening a birthday present, opening a letter with sad news (a friend is moving away) followed by happy news (you can go to visit).

Other aspects of the English PoS covered

Writing – 1a, b, c; 2b, c.

Reference to photocopiable sheet

Photocopiable page 129 provides a set of pictures showing a range of situations. These will stimulate discussion and allow children the opportunity to speculate on what the characters might be saying.

WHO OWNS WHAT?

To develop reasoning skills by finding links between people and objects; attentive listening.

†† *Groups of three to five.*

🕐 *45 minutes.*

Key background information

The task in this activity is to assign the various objects on the photocopiable sheet to three people who have been described to the children. Some of the objects and people are obviously linked, while others require discussion and decision making. This matching exercise requires children to make and justify decisions.

Resources needed

One copy per group of photocopiable page 130; chalkboard; scissors (optional). For the extension activity – writing materials.

What to do

Give each group a copy of photocopiable page 130. If you wish, the group can cut it up into individual items. This will enable them to allocate the items physically to their owners.

Read out the potted descriptions of the three characters (see below), writing just their names on the board. Give the children some time to absorb the information. Explain the activity, when you have read the character descriptions, and then tell the groups to begin sorting out the various items. Explain that for some of the items there is no right or wrong answer and it is up to the children to put forward a good case. Some objects – the packet of crisps, for instance – do not have an obvious owner and a process of elimination will have to be used.

> *Character 1* Mr Thompson is a teacher of maths at a secondary school. He is married with a new baby. He is interested in science, astronomy and hill walking.
> *Character 2* Kelly is ten years old and loves pop music. She is keen on sport and hates eating and drinking junk food. She always walks to school.
> *Character 3* Mrs Jebson is 78 years old. She is very fit, believes in a healthy diet and still leads an active life. She often wins prizes for the flowers and vegetables she grows in her garden. She has seven grandchildren aged from five to fifteen. In her house are many objects collected over a long life.

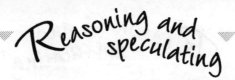

After a while, read out the descriptions again and allow a further few minutes for second thoughts.

When all the groups have finished, discuss the objects with the whole class. If any of the groups have reached different conclusions, ask them to justify their decisions.

Suggestion(s) for extension

A more challenging activity is to provide a list of characters, for example a farmer, a pop star, an alien, a builder, a doctor. Ask the groups to make a list of items each character is likely to own. Alternatively, ask each group to decide on a character of their choice before making a list of items that this character might possess. This could be a real person – a class member, for example. They can then read out their lists, an item at a time, and ask the other groups to guess who or what their character is.

Suggestion(s) for support

Ensure that all children know what the objects are. This should be done through group discussion, but the groups may ask if they cannot identify some of the objects.

Assessment opportunities

Correct allocation of items demonstrates reasoning. More important is to assess the quality of negotiation and discussion activity taking place in the groups.

Display/performance ideas

Much interesting work can be done on collecting. Children (and many adults, of course) are enthusiastic collectors. Children collect football cards, models, interestingly shaped

erasers – even bus tickets! Ask children to display their collections, and say what they find interesting about their collection and the process of collecting. Individual children can prepare a 'My life through objects' display, with objects or pictures of objects that have been very important in the child's life. Possibilities are a favourite teddy bear or toy; a well-read book; a memento from a holiday or trip; a special gift. Adults can be invited to show their own collections.

Reference to photocopiable sheet

Photocopiable page 130 presents a range of items which belong to one or more of the characters, descriptions of whom have been read out to the children. The children discuss 'who owns what' and provide the reasoning behind their decisions.

▣ KEEP SAFE!

To use deduction to spot dangers in a 'safety first' picture.
†† *Group or pair discussion and writing.*
🕐 *20 minutes.*

Previous skills/knowledge needed

Some background knowledge on home safety would be useful, or this activity can introduce a topic on this subject, perhaps as part of the science curriculum.

Key background information

This activity assesses children's abilities to recognise common dangers in the home. Some are obvious, but others have need of a deeper insight into dangerous possibilities, and children will require a more complex understanding of what might happen – the curtain close to the cooker, for example, or the loose mat on the floor. Some children might note that there is no smoke alarm or fire extinguisher fitted in the kitchen!

Resources needed

One copy per group or pair of photocopiable page 131; chalkboard; writing materials. For the support activity – word bank (optional).

What to do

With a confident class, give out the copies of photocopiable page 131 to the groups or pairs without preliminary discussion. Ask them to discuss it and to list as many dangers as they can find. Ensure that they follow the usual routine for group work – appointing a chair and a scribe. (See Introduction, 'Collaborative skills – groups', page 8.)

Some classes might benefit from a general discussion on safety in the home, before the materials are distributed. An alternative approach is to use the picture for class discussion, prompting where necessary with questions such

as 'Is there anything missing from the kitchen?' 'What might the toddler do?' If you are working as a class, list the dangers on the board as they are found.

Suggestion(s) for extension
Extend the groups' abilities by asking them to draw up a safety-first plan for a kitchen or another room. Ask them to make up ten 'golden rules' for kitchen safety, based on the picture, or for other places such as a living room, a swimming pool, an infant classroom or a playground.

Suggestion(s) for support
Children may have problems with vocabulary and spelling; there are difficult words involved, such as 'extinguisher', 'boiling saucepan', 'electrical socket'. If required, prepare a vocabulary list to give out to less able groups only.

Assessment opportunities
Look particularly at how well the dangers are expressed in writing by the scribe. Some explanations might be quite extended and require the ability to organise complex information into clear, simple words, presented as a short talk to the class.

Opportunities for IT
Show the children how to create a multimedia, interactive 'Keep safe!' presentation. If the picture on photocopiable page 131 is scanned and then placed on to a computer screen page, each of the dangers can be identified by the children and linked to another screen. For example, clicking on the loose mat will take the user to a screen which has a picture of the loose mat, the reason why it is dangerous and what to do to make it safe. Another picture or arrow will take the user back to the main picture page so that he or she can

look for another danger. Let the children work in pairs, and allocate one danger to each pair. Ask the children to create a screen which will be linked to the master picture. The children could record the explanation as a sound-clip, using a microphone attached to the computer.

Display ideas
Enlarge photocopiable page 131 and use as the centre of a 'safety first' display, with the dangers written out and linked to the picture with cotton thread. The golden rules can be developed into a poster.

Produce a similar display for 'safety first' in the other places suggested in the extension activity.

Other aspects of the English PoS covered
Writing – 1a, b, c; 2b.

Reference to photocopiable sheet
Photocopiable page 131 offers a typical 'Safety in the home' picture. The class are asked to discuss the picture, in pairs or groups, and then list all the possible dangers depicted in it.

ANIMAL QUESTIONS

To reason by asking questions.

†† *Whole class.*

⏱ *Can be a short filler activity, or a more extended activity.*

Key background information
We learn by asking appropriate questions. Simple twenty questions type games are very valuable because they teach the process of narrowing down by elimination. With animals, a question such as 'How many legs has it got?' will rule out a whole group of animals.

Usually, twenty questions insists on 'yes/no' answers. In this game, this rule does not apply, but all questions must begin with the words 'where', 'when' or 'how'. (Note that 'what' is not allowed because the answers give too much away.) Children will have to think very carefully about the phrasing of their questions.

Resources needed

Pictures of animals are useful but not essential.

What to do

Ask one child either to look at a picture of an animal or to decide on an animal of his or her own. The rest of the class should then take it in turns to ask questions beginning with 'where', 'when' or 'how'. If the child with the picture does not know the answer, you can help out. Possible questions are:

▲ Where does it live?
▲ How many legs does it have?
▲ When does it sleep?
▲ Where does it feed?

  Let the questioning continue until someone thinks that they know what the animal is. They should then stand up. (Calling out is not allowed.) If the correct answer is given, the game stops and the correct guesser chooses the next animal. If the guess is wrong, the guesser sits down and the game continues. Allow only one guess per person. Put a time limit (three minutes is about right) on each round.

Suggestion(s) for extension

To make the game more difficult, insist that 'when', 'where' and 'how' are used in strict rotation. Even more challenging is to use the same game for things other than animals.

Suggestion(s) for support

Some children may find it difficult to answer the questions, particularly with unusual animals. Try to ensure that such children can cope. A good choice might be an animal which they have for a pet, or a very common animal – cat, dog, cow and so on. Alternatively, the questions can be answered by a group or pair working together in consultation, perhaps with a support teacher.

Assessment opportunities

Focus on the quality of the questions as well as the confidence in answering them. Watch out also for understanding of the protocols of class discussion. Be aware of children who listen attentively to the answers given, then pose appropriate questions.

Display ideas

Write out the questions and answers on a piece of paper. Then use this to form a lift-up flap, covering a picture of the object. Ask observers to try to guess what the picture will be before they lift the flap.

IF ONLY...

To use speculation in a more imaginative context.
†† *Class discussion, followed by pair discussion and writing.*
🕐 *30 minutes, followed by time for redrafting.*

Key background information

This activity encourages children to stretch their imaginations by speculating on 'What if...?' or 'If only...' It does not matter how unlikely the situation which they devise is. Many children find the leap from logical, 'straight-line' thinking to discovery through imagination difficult. This activity is a way through that barrier.

Resources needed

Chalkboard; writing materials.

What to do

Introduce the idea outlined above to the class as a whole, with some 'What if...?' and 'If only...' ideas of your own. Possibilities are:

▲ What if it never rained again?
▲ What if clouds were made of ice-cream?
▲ If only every day were a holiday.
▲ If only money grew on trees.
▲ What if the school were invaded by giant spiders?
▲ If only animals could talk.
▲ If only I ran the country.
▲ If only we could fly.
▲ What if we shrank to the size of an ant?
▲ What if all grown-ups disappeared for a day?

  Encourage the children to brainstorm their own ideas, letting their imaginations roam freely in thinking about their 'What if...?' and 'If only...' ideas. Write the children's ideas in note-form on the board. Ask the children to choose the most interesting or unusual ideas, and then, working in pairs or groups, to brainstorm these ideas further, thinking about what might happen and what they would do if the situation ever occurred.

  The brainstormed ideas can then be developed into a finished piece of writing, either a poem or a story. If the children are not confident with poetry writing, guidance may be needed on finding a suitable structure for the writing. One possibility is to repeat a line, such as 'If only the Moon were made of cheese' every few lines, to create a running chorus. This pattern can be suggested in the class brainstorm.

Suggestion(s) for extension

In pairs, ask the children to think about more serious and plausible 'What if...?' or 'If only...' ideas: 'If only there were peace in the world', 'If only there were enough food in the world' and 'What if the school had £1000 to spend?' These can be worked on as described above.

SPEAKING AND
LISTENING

Suggestion(s) for support

This sort of imaginative thinking is an area where less able children can often excel, as learning difficulties are rarely a bar to imagination. Much guidance will be needed with the writing stage, however. Think carefully about your pairing arrangements in the class.

Assessment opportunities

In the finished writing, look for ideas that surprise you, as a reader. Although this is a writing assessment, the quality of the writing will depend on the quality of the speaking and listening that took place. Most importantly, monitor the quality of the paired discussion. Look for genuine sharing of ideas rather than domination by one partner.

Opportunities for IT

Let the children use a word processor to write their 'What if...?' or 'If only...' poems. Simple illustrations taken from clip-art collections, drawn with an art package or scanned from their own line drawings, can be added to enhance the appearance of the finished text.

Display/performance ideas

The completed poems or stories, perhaps ones that have been word-processed in the IT activity, can be made into small books, with the title 'What if...? or If only...' on the front cover. Alternatively, poems can be performed. Allow time for practice and rehearsal of performances.

Other aspects of the English PoS covered

Writing – 1a, b, c; 2b; 3c.

YES/NO GAME

To develop skills of speculating by a process of elimination.

†† *Whole class, followed by groups.*

🕐 *A short activity for odd moments, but can be expanded into a longer game.*

Key background information

This activity is a version of twenty questions and complements the activity 'Animal questions'. By asking 'yes/no' questions the final answer is arrived at by a process of elimination. The skill is to think of a broad range of questions, in order to eliminate as many options as possible. Children are inclined to ask questions which are too specific ('Is it a pencil?') rather than general ones ('Is it a man-made object?').

Resources needed

A box; a range of objects which are small enough to fit in the box individually (the items should be relatively familiar ones). For the support activity – writing materials.

What to do

First, try the game informally with the whole class. Produce the box with one object concealed within and explain the rules – guessing the object using 'yes/no' questions only. If necessary, explain what a 'yes/no' question is. For example, 'What colour is it?' is an illegal question, but 'Is it more than one colour?' is acceptable. Insist on the children putting their hands up to ask questions.

Play the game until the object is guessed or the class and yourself weary of it! Review the playing of the game, pointing out the differences between specific and broad questions, and stressing the importance of listening to other people's questions and the answers given. (Often children will be entirely focused on the question they are about to ask, and repeat questions already asked by others.) Now try a second object. (You may need a second box, unless by some sleight of hand you are able to refill the first box without being seen.)

Run the game once more, this time limiting the number of questions by allowing only one question per child. Encourage every child to ask at least one question.

Suggestion(s) for extension

Once the class are familiar with the game, allow them to play it in groups. Answering the questions is a challenging task, as some questions are very difficult to answer!

Suggestion(s) for support

This is a game of reasoning, and some children may find it difficult to come up with effective questions. Encourage the questioners to use paper and pencil to aid short-term memory. This will allow them to note down vital facts, and to think up more questions while waiting for their turn to ask.

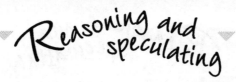
Assessment opportunities

This is a useful activity for assessing how well children can use and remember clues, and work through a reasoning sequence.

Opportunities for IT

Once the game has been played with a single object, the children can use a branching database to create an electronic key for identifying a number of different objects within the box. This type of database differs from conventional ones in that the children must teach the software about the different shapes by phrasing questions that can only be answered by 'yes' or 'no'. Answering 'yes' to a question leads in one direction, 'no' in another. The resulting key can be used by other children to identify any object in the set of shapes. For example:

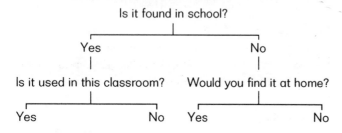

Is it found in school?

Yes — Is it used in this classroom? — Yes / No

No — Would you find it at home? — Yes / No

Organise the activity with children working in small groups, each group having a limited range of objects at first. A key part of the activity is to decide on the first question, which will provide a good basis for splitting the whole set. Different groups of children can try out their database with other groups to test how easy it is to use and how accurate the answers are.

Display ideas

If a tape is made of the questions and answers they can be transcribed to make an interesting display. List the questions and answers, then ask the reader to guess what the object is. The object (or a picture of it) can be 'hidden', only to be revealed once the reader has made a guess or 'given up'.

Other aspects of the English PoS covered

Writing – 2b.

A GARDEN FOR A VISUALLY IMPAIRED PERSON

To develop group planning skills.

✝✝ *Groups of three to five.*

🕐 *45 minutes, or can be extended into a longer project.*

Previous skills/knowledge needed

The children will need to be familiar with the tasks of chairing and scribing, and general group organisation. Work on scale drawing is essential. If there is a school garden, this could be a useful starting point, looking at widths of paths, sizes of flower-beds and so on.

Key background information

This activity requires groups to work together in quite a sophisticated way on a design project, the object of which is to produce plans for a garden for a visually impaired person.

An additional valuable outcome of the project is a deeper understanding of the needs and capabilities of visually impaired people.

Preparation

It would be useful to familiarise yourself with the specific needs of visually impaired people: level surfaces, handrails, auditory and tactile clues such as different paving materials, and so on. If possible, make contact with a visually impaired person who would be prepared to come and talk to the class.

Resources needed

A3 squared writing paper; seed and garden catalogues; chalkboard; writing and drawing materials.

What to do

Outline the project, starting with a discussion on what a visual impairment is. (The term covers a range of sight deficits including blindness.) Give the dimensions of the proposed garden, say 50 × 20 metres, and explain that each group is expected to produce a written report and a plan. Subjects for the discussion might be 'What a visually impaired person would particularly enjoy in a garden' and 'Safety' (for example, water adds a sound element to a garden, but it must be safe). Obviously the involvement of a visually impaired person, as a class visitor, would add an extra dimension to the project. The children would need to prepare a range of questions in advance of an interview.

Set the groups to work. Encourage the following stages, perhaps by listing them on the board:

▲ brainstorming ideas;

▲ making a list of requirements;

▲ drafting rough plans, including paths, flower-beds and so on (refer the children to the garden catalogues you have collected);

▲ using squared paper to try out ideas;

▲ producing a final report with a carefully drawn scale plan and written material.

While the group work is continuing, troubleshoot by visiting each group in turn.

Suggestion(s) for extension

More able groups can research the project in greater detail, finding out about scented varieties of plants, different surfacing materials, 'touch' plants such as trees with

interesting bark, varied foliage (no spines!) and so on. Allow such groups more time.

Suggestion(s) for support

Less able groups will benefit from the involvement of a support teacher. Alternatively, such groups might be asked to produce a less accurate plan, not necessarily to scale.

Assessment opportunities

The groups as a whole can be assessed by the final outcomes. Observe the group dynamics in action as you monitor their work; the discussion work that takes place is more important than the written/drawn plans.

Opportunities for IT

If possible, obtain a CD-ROM on garden plants to enable children to carry out research and gather information about plants which would be appropriate in a garden for a visually impaired person because they are scented.

A drawing package can be used to help the children design the garden. If the package is set up with a background grid selected it makes it easier for the children to draw their garden to scale. It might be possible for children to use specific garden design software for this activity. Children could use an art package to 'paint' a picture of each flower-bed in the style of a particular artist, such as Monet or Van Gogh, using the art package tools.

Display ideas

These plans make attractive displays. The final scale drawings can be set next to the written reports.

Other aspects of the English PoS covered

Reading – 1a, b; 2c, d.
Writing – 1a, b, c; 2a, b.

CRISIS!

To develop reasoning and problem-solving in an amusing and imaginative way.

†† *Group or pair discussion and reporting back; whole class listening.*

🕐 *20 minutes plus presentation time.*

Previous skills/knowledge needed

The children will require experience in group work or pair work.

Key background information

This activity requires children, working together, to devise improbable solutions to unlikely crises. It requires quick thinking and reasoning, but in this case the more unlikely and outrageous the result the better! Many children find it difficult to give free range to their imagination, and this exercise encourages this. The idea is similar to that featured in *The Eighteenth Emergency* by Betsy Byars (Puffin). Children would enjoy listening to a reading of this book or extracts from it, and it would be an effective, though not essential, introduction to this activity.

Preparation

A number of possible 'crises' are suggested below, but you may prefer to prepare others in advance.

Resources needed

A copy of *The Eighteenth Emergency* by Betsy Byars (optional).

What to do

Put the children into pairs or groups. Explain that they are going to have to solve some serious crises. With as grave a face as possible, tell them that a nearby school was recently attacked by a rampaging elephant, but the school was saved by two quick-thinking children who rushed to a nearby baker's shop for a large sackful of buns. They made a trail of these back to the zoo. Elephants cannot resist buns, so this one followed the trail, eating the buns on the way. When it got back, it had eaten so many buns it fell asleep...

Explain that it is important to be prepared for any emergency, however unlikely. What, for example, would you do if a petrol tanker thundered down the hill out of control? (Answer: Luckily there is another lorry close by loaded with cushions. Bravely, you drive in front of the speeding petrol tanker, while a friend in the back throws the cushions in the path of the lorry. The huge piles of cushions slow down the tanker and bring it to a halt just in time...)

Work through one of the crises listed below, with the class as a whole. Then give the groups or pairs ten minutes to discuss and solve a further crisis. You could give the whole class the same crisis, which will result in a range of solutions, or each pair or group could have a problem of their own. This allows you to set more challenging problems to particularly imaginative groups.

▲ You are bound hand and foot to a chair. In ten minutes the dynamite will explode...

▲ You drop your aunt's best china plate. It breaks in two...

▲ You are a postman. A savage dog has you cornered...

▲ You fall into a river. The alligators approach...

▲ A gust of wind slams the door of your house locked shut with you outside. Inside, the chip pan starts to smoke...

▲ You reach a wide river. The enemy are close behind. Unfortunately, you can't swim...

▲ You are alone and lost in a dark cave. Suddenly, your torch goes out...

▲ A tall building is on fire. You are stranded on the roof...

▲ You are flying an aeroplane. A passing seagull has pecked a hole in your fuel tank. The engine starts to splutter. You knew you should have brought that parachute...

After ten minutes, ask the groups to present their solutions.

The same approach can be used for solving real problems: saving energy in the school, solving local traffic problems, and so on. In this case, you will be looking for serious rather than comic solutions.

Suggestion(s) for extension
Many children may enjoy devising their own crises, for themselves or for the class.

Suggestion(s) for support
Ensure that all children have an opportunity to present their ideas. This is an appropriate activity for a support group to work together with you or a support teacher on one of the less challenging activities listed in 'What to do'.

Assessment opportunities
Examining the children's solutions will enable you to note how well they have used their imagination, the effectiveness with which the solutions have been presented, and how convincing the children's solutions have been, even when they have incorporated very silly ideas!

Opportunities for IT
Ask the children to use a word processor or desktop publishing package to present their final solutions to the crisis, adding illustrations drawn with an art package, taken from clip-art collections or scanned from their own line drawings.

Display ideas
The problems and solutions can be written up, with appropriate artwork, to make an attractive and amusing display.

Other aspects of the English PoS covered
Writing 1a, b, c; 2b; 3a, c.

Opinion and persuasion

The aim of this chapter is to encourage children to offer their own opinions in an effective way, and to use persuasive language to convince others of a point of view. On the listening side, a number of activities encourage children to beware persuasion when it is inappropriate (by peer pressure or commercial advertising, for instance) and suggest strategies for coping with this. There is also work on listening to and respecting the opinions of others, and on exploring personal feelings and difficulties in an open way.

More than any other chapter, this one is all about self-confidence. To put forward a point of view, to have strong opinions, implies that children value themselves, and have the confidence to 'stand out from the crowd'. At this age, children's opinions on major issues such as pollution, cruelty, and right and wrong may not be well informed or objective, but they should be encouraged to have opinions, and to know that those opinions will be listened to and respected by others.

Listening to and accepting the opinions of others is a difficult task for children. Doing this is a three-part process: listening to the views of others, evaluating those views and, if appropriate, modifying the listener's own opinions to take account of what has been said. In a speaking and listening activity, children can be so busy thinking about what they are to say that they do not listen to others. This problem is addressed by telling children in advance that a response of some sort is required.

SPEAKING AND
LISTENING

TIME CAPSULE

To put forward points of view in a group discussion.
♦♦ *Class discussion, then groups of three to five.*
🕐 *Open ended.*

Previous skills/knowledge needed

Children will need to have had practice in group work, particularly in negotiating and reporting-back skills.

Key background information

Time capsules provide a wonderful opportunity for discussion and argument, and for putting forward points of view and negotiating. In this activity each group decides which ten items to include in their time capsule, to be buried and dug up by future generations.

Resources needed

Shoeboxes and real time-capsule objects for a display (optional); writing materials.

What to do

Start the activity with a class discussion on time capsules and their purposes. These are:
▲ to show future generations what life was like at the time the capsule was buried;
▲ to preserve objects typical of our time for future generations.

Explain that time capsules have to be quite small. The children will be choosing ten items and these will all have to fit into a space which is the size of a shoebox. Point out that some items – compact discs, videos – require machines to play them and these may not be available in the future.

Form the children into groups. Suggest that they begin with a quiet individual brainstorm during which each person in the group draws up his or her own list of ten items for the time capsule. The groups should then discuss and negotiate a final, joint list of ten items. Discourage the groups from allowing each member of the group two or three unargued choices each. Suggest that the time capsule might be linked to a specific place or event – the school perhaps, or a special occasion such as a centenary. The children may like to think of a specific year in which the box is to be opened.

Allow around 15 minutes for the discussion, then ask the groups to report back to the class, giving their choices and justifying them. Rather than ask one child to do this, ask that each child in the group announces some of the objects and explains why they were chosen for inclusion.

A class discussion can now follow, to decide on ten items drawn from the groups' ideas for a class time capsule. If the school is having building work carried out – an extension, for example – consider the possibility of making a real time capsule.

Suggestion(s) for extension

A more challenging activity is to consider what objects might be sent out into space, to inform an alien race about ourselves. (School reference books will supply information about the Voyager space probe, and what it contained.) Ask the groups to design their own space probes. This is a more complex task, as objects such as coins or items of clothing will be recognisable to a future generation but may not mean much to an alien!

Suggestion(s) for support

Monitor the groups carefully, to ensure less confident children are given a fair hearing.

Assessment opportunities

Look for real imagination shown in the choice of items, and the strength of the arguments put forward.

Display ideas

Time capsules make an attractive display. Children could either draw pictures of them, with items they would like to include, or a real time capsule could be made using a shoe box with objects placed in it. Include writing on how and why the choices were made. A similar display can be made for space probes.

Other aspects of the English PoS covered

Writing – 1a, b, c; 2b.
Reading – 1b.

◇ ▣ CLEANING THE CAR

To build confidence in using persuasive language.

†† *Pairs.*

⊕ *10 minutes per pair.*

Key background information

Some may argue that children are masters of persuasion, particularly with parents, and they need no further encouragement! This drama activity looks at the way children 'work' on their parents, and suggests a range of themes for improvisation in pairs. As with other activities based on family situations and relationships, it is intended as a light-hearted activity. It is recognised that in some classes there will be families who are not well off, and many children whose parent or parents do not have a car to clean. In this case, a sensitive alternative situation should be found. The ideas on photocopiable page 133 include many that are not money based.

Preparation

Make copies of photocopiable page 132, one for each pair. You will also need to make copies of photocopiable page 133 and cut out the sections.

Resources needed

One copy per pair of photocopiable page 132; copies of photocopiable page 133 cut into separate sections; chalkboard (optional); writing materials.

What to do

Start with a class discussion on 'how to persuade parents'. Allow the children to relate anecdotes about times when they were successful or unsuccessful. Include stories of your own – these may be from your childhood, or accounts of how you persuaded a partner, friend or colleague to do something which he or she did not really want to do!

Ask the children to work in pairs. Give out copies of photocopiable page 132, and ask them to prepare a performance of the script and then improvise a conclusion. The sheet is designed to allow children to adopt their own gender.

When they are ready, ask one pair to perform their version to the class.

Now give each pair one slip from photocopiable page 133, and ask them to prepare an improvised performance based on the situation they have been given. Other situations may suggest themselves from the introductory discussion and you could prepare appropriate slips for those situations.

The activity can be followed up with script or story writing. Persuading parents can be an effective theme for poetry writing. If the 'cleaning the car' script is felt to be inappropriate, pairs can be asked to develop their own opening script. Alternatively, one can be produced on the board by the whole class during a brainstorming session.

Suggestion(s) for extension

A follow-up discussion could focus on the differences between persuasion and blackmail. Children sometimes nag and nag until parents give in out of desperation. Is this blackmail or honest persuasion?

Suggestion(s) for support

Performing from a script is a difficult task for some children. They may find it easier to perform only the improvised section. Allow time for rehearsal. If possible, support less able children by special attention to pairings and, where possible, giving teacher/support teacher help while the improvisation is being developed. The addition of a third character in the script – two children and one parent – can help too.

Assessment opportunities

Look for evidence of children working effectively with a partner, using imaginative talk spontaneously, and speaking and performing effectively to an audience.

Opportunities for IT

Encourage the children to write scripts for their improvised performances, using a word processor or desktop publishing package. If children use a word processor, show them how to use formatting commands such as tabs and hanging indents to lay out their writing in the form of a dialogue. Emphasise that they should not use the space bar to move text around the screen. Hanging indents are an important facility to use to

SPEAKING AND LISTENING

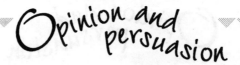

ensure that the spoken text wraps around in the correct place and does not go back to the start of the line.

If children use a desktop publishing package, they can set out two columns and type directly into the columns. Some word processors have a 'table' facility which can be used to produce a similar effect. This method is probably the easiest for the children to use once the columns have been set up. The word processor provides the opportunity to print out several versions, with children being given updated copies when revisions have been made.

Performance ideas

The completed improvisations can be rehearsed or scripted for performance to other classes or the school.

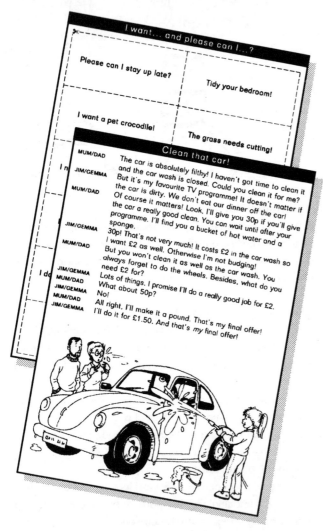

Other aspects of the English PoS covered

Reading – 1c; 2b.

Writing – 1a, b, c; 2b.

Reference to photocopiable sheets

Photocopiable page 132 provides a script which the children use in their performance, adding their own improvised conclusion. They prepare another improvised performance for the situation allocated to them on photocopiable page 133.

INTERVIEWING

To look closely at the techniques of interviewing, and put them into practice.

✝✝ *Paired role-play; class listening and discussion.*

🕐 *45 minutes.*

Key background information

Being able to interview is a key skill, but something children are generally not very skilled at. They will usually prepare a few questions in advance, but will rarely be confident enough to extend the interview by asking supplementary questions. This activity looks closely at the process of interviewing, firstly through class discussion, and then by listening to a professional interviewer on radio or television and discussing the techniques used. These techniques can be used in a general situation when the class is asking a visitor questions (see the activity 'Off the cuff', page 29).

Preparation

You will need a tape of a radio or television interview for this activity. This can be on any topic, but it is best to select one that will be of interest to the class – the environment, say – rather than an interview with a politician who may be evasive. This is an exercise in effective interviewing, not in avoiding answering questions!

Resources needed

A recording of an interview (see 'Preparation'); a cassette or video player and television. (You will need to ensure that your school or LEA has an Educational Recording Agency licence.)

What to do

Set up a small role-play activity in which one child plays an 'expert' (this should be a topic of special interest to the interviewee) and another a television interviewer.

Now play the tape of the professional interview. Discuss the differences.

The discussion should bring out:

▲ how interviewers ask supplementary questions based on the answers received;

▲ how interviewers ask for further clarification of points that were unclear;

▲ how interviewers ask their subjects to justify the statements they have made.

You may need to prompt children by asking questions yourself.

Now repeat the role-play exercise with two different children. Discuss how effectively the new interviewer is using the techniques discussed.

Suggestion(s) for extension

Working individually or in pairs, children could interview an adult connected with the school: the headteacher, another teacher, caretaker and so on. The interviews can be recorded on tape or video, and transcriptions made.

Suggestion(s) for support

This is quite a challenging task for less confident children. An additional activity is to pair all of the children for an interview role-play, taking it in turns to interview each other. Being interviewed is probably easier than interviewing!

Assessment opportunities

Note how much children have learned from the class discussion and how well they are able to put this into practice.

FINDING OUT WHAT PEOPLE THINK

To develop skills in group planning and interviewing.
†† *Whole class then group work, followed by individual or pair interviewing.*
🕓 *Open ended.*

Key background information

The task in this activity is to prepare a questionnaire seeking opinions on a chosen topic, then use this to interview members of the school. It mirrors the professional approach to opinion polling:
▲ designing a questionnaire;

▲ validating it with a small sample;
▲ ensuring an appropriate cross-section of those responding;
▲ processing the data obtained.

A range of speaking and listening skills are developed in the activity, both in the planning stage and in carrying out the survey.

Resources needed

If possible, a selection of 'multiple-choice' questionnaires; one copy per child or group of photocopiable page 134; writing materials.

What to do

To provide some preparatory work on designing questionnaires, give each child a copy of photocopiable page 134. Work through the questions on the sheet with the class, asking them to raise their hands to the answers they agree with. Demonstrate entering the figures on your own copy. Talk about the results of your survey. Explain that the best way to find out information that can be easily processed is to provide multiple-choice questions. A question on favourite types of television programmes, for example, should offer a range of various programmes with tick boxes. If possible, show other multiple-choice questionnaires, either commercial ones or educational tests.

Put the children into groups of three or four. Ask the children to prepare a questionnaire, using the model of 'Your town' on the photocopiable sheet. You will need to discuss topics for the questionnaire. The topic may arise out of work currently under way with the class, or can cover such things as aspects of the school, television programmes, favourite food and healthy living.

Once the questionnaire is prepared, the groups will need to find interviewees – members of the class, other children in the school, staff. Ask the groups to work through the following process:
▲ Design the questionnaire.
▲ Try it out on one person.
▲ Talk about how successfully the questionnaire worked and whether changes are needed.
▲ Think about who your target is (Equal numbers of boys and girls? Children of all ages or just one class? Will adults be included? Is the questionnaire designed to show differences, perhaps between adults and children, boys and girls, children of different ages?).
▲ Make copies of your questionnaire – one for each interviewer/pair of interviewers (offer help at this stage by photocopying if required).
▲ Carry out your survey (the group can split up into individuals or pairs for the interviewing).

The 'Your town' questionnaire is designed for a verbal rather than a written response, and one sheet can be used for a number of interviews. The results can be found by adding up the ticks.

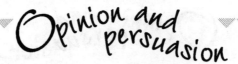

Opinion and persuasion

The information acquired should be used by the groups to produce some graph work, perhaps using computer graphics, and a spoken presentation to the class which should involve an explanation of how they went about designing, modifying and carrying out their survey.

Suggestion(s) for extension
This is a challenging activity. Allow the most able children to have responsibility for leading the groups.

Suggestion(s) for support
Listen in to each group and ensure everyone is involved in the activity. Be prepared to offer help and advice when they are required. Groups finding the activity difficult could work on a simplified survey such as the favourite flavour of crisps, where there is a (relatively!) limited choice.

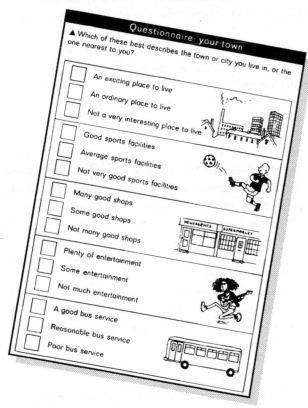

Assessment opportunities
Observe how effectively individuals in the class work as a member of a group.

Opportunities for IT
Results from the questionnaire can be analysed using a computer database. With some databases, such as Junior Pinpoint, it is possible to create a questionnaire on the computer screen, print out copies, and after the questionnaires have been completed, to return to the computer and input the results on the same page. The children will need to think carefully about how to ask questions which will produce answers that are consistent enough in style for them to be used for comparison.

Display ideas
The data can be displayed, perhaps as part of ongoing work in mathematics.

Other aspects of the English PoS covered
Writing – 1a, c; 2a, b.

Reference to photocopiable sheet
Photocopiable page 134 provides a model for designing questionnaires. It can also be used as a 'ready-made' questionnaire on local issues.

MAKING EXCUSES

To build confidence in discussing persuasive language and relating anecdotes.
†† *Whole class discussion, then pairs.*
⏲ *Open ended.*

Key background information
Children recognise that they are sometimes guilty of outrageous and unbelievable excuses and are happy to laugh at themselves. This activity initiates discussion on 'my worst excuses' and can lead to writing or role-play activities.

Resources needed
Writing materials.

What to do
Initiate a class discussion on excuses with an account of a time when you made an outrageous excuse, perhaps as a child. Then read the poem 'Where's that homework?' below.

Where's that homework?
'Please Miss, I left it on the bus.'
'Please Miss, my dog chewed it up.'
'Please Miss, I posted it in the letter-box with my mum's letters.'
'Please Miss, I left it on the beach when I was swimming and a huge wave washed it away.'
'Please Miss, it was stolen by an international gang of homework thieves.'
'Please Miss, my house was invaded by aliens last night and they took it off in a flying saucer.'
'Please Miss... I just forgot.'

During the discussion, encourage the telling of real events rather than fantasy. Common situations that you could suggest are:
▲ going home with torn clothes;
▲ losing important things;
▲ forgetting to do something;
▲ breaking something valuable.

SPEAKING AND LISTENING

Encourage the children to think of a time when their parents have made up excuses about things which they have or have not done. If appropriate, extend the discussion to consider the importance of truthfulness.

To conclude the activity, ask the children to work in pairs and relate their own excuse anecdotes, with their partner scribing. Use the resultant material for story or poetry writing, or for scripting. The poem 'Where's that homework?' is a useful writing model, substituting 'Please Miss' with 'Please Mum/Dad' and so on. The material can, of course, extend into total fantasy at this stage, in the same way that the poem becomes more and more outrageous.

Suggestion(s) for extension.
More able and confident children can be set difficult challenges to 'get out of' by thinking up outrageous excuses. Remember, though, the importance of real experience as material for writing. Challenge children by asking them to relate remembered incidents amusingly and effectively. Allow time for preparation.

Suggestion(s) for support
Ensure that all children play their full part. See notes on supporting class discussion in the Introduction ('Working as a class', page 9).

Assessment opportunities
This activity presents an opportunity to assess both individual confidence in joining in a class discussion, and also how successful the children are at 'convincing' an audience with the most implausible stories.

Opportunities for IT
Ask the children to use a word processor to write up their 'most terrible' excuse. Emphasise the need to focus on the presentation of their work, and make it interesting to read, using different fonts, styles or sizes for the text. Suggest that they could add borders to improve the appearance of their finished work.

Display/performance ideas
A 'terrible excuses' display will provide stimuli for interesting talking points. Ask each child to write out his or her most terrible excuse, and then display the writing, perhaps accompanying each one with a picture of the child who made it. The best excuses can be developed into script writing and drama work, for presentation to the class or other children in the school.

Other aspects of the English PoS covered
Writing – 1a, b, c; 2b.

THE ARK GAME

To develop confidence in persuasive speech.
†† *Individual note making, then presentation to the class.*
🕐 *30–40 minutes*

Key background information
This is a version of the balloon game, in which a sinking balloon is heading for disaster! The only possibility for survival is for someone to jump (or be pushed) out! Each person in the balloon therefore has to argue why he or she should be saved. In this version each child assumes the persona of an animal, and has to argue his or her relative worth, to try to convince a present-day Noah to allow him or her on to the ark. Children will have to show their ingenuity in defending the indefensible – animals such as cockroaches and poisonous snakes may not be the most popular candidates for admittance to the ark.

Preparation
Prepare some animal cards. These can be made by cutting out animal pictures from magazines and supplements and mounting them on card. Alternatively, cards with just the name of the animal written on them would suffice.

Resources needed
Animal cards; reference books (if required); writing materials; photocopiable assessment page 135 (as required).

Suggestion(s) for extension

An alternative to choosing animals by picking them out randomly is to arrange for the more capable children to be given the most difficult animals to defend – animals which may have unpleasant characteristics and are not particularly appealing.

Suggestion(s) for support

Some children may need support in finding information and preparing notes. Try to ensure that these children have familiar animals to deal with, such as pets, or ones which are obviously useful, such as farmyard animals.

Assessment opportunities

This is a good opportunity to observe how effectively individual children speak and perform to an audience. It is an appropriate activity for summative assessment and a photocopiable record sheet is provided on page 135.

Opinion and persuasion	
Name: _____ Age: _____	
Class: _____ Date of assessment: _____	
Comments on skill in persuasion and giving opinions:	
Can use persuasive language effectively.	
Can give information in a logical and ordered way.	
Can offer and justify opinions.	
Can speak with fluency, confidence and awareness of audience.	
Can use standard English effectively.	
Can speak with awareness of standard grammatical constructions.	
Can speak with clear diction and appropriate intonation.	
Can organise a presentation in an effective way.	
General comments:	

What to do

Give out the cards at random, or ask children to pick them out of a hat. Explain the rules of the Ark game: there is a limited number of places on the ark; each animal has to explain why it should be allowed on; the final decision will be made by the class voting, but no one can vote for themselves.

Give the children time to make notes on their own animal, using reference books if required. They should then present their case before Noah, represented by the class. The arguments should not be based exclusively on the factual information in reference books – children should be encouraged to be imaginative as well! Allow the class to vote for a maximum of, say, six animals. The animals with the most votes will be allowed on to the ark.

A further development is to ask a child to play the part of Noah, who then has to explain to a particular animal why there is no room for it!

The game can lead to interesting written work in which children argue the case for themselves as the various animals. Writing, in which unpleasant animals try and put an attractive gloss on themselves, can work well as 'first person' poetry. Such poems could start off like this:

I'm a grey rat.
People hate me, but
I'm not all bad...

This can be followed by all the positive aspects of rats, real or imaginary!

Opportunities for IT

Ask the children to present their reasoning as to why animals should be saved by writing using a word processor or desktop publishing package. The final versions can then be used for a class display or bound to make a class book.

Alternatively, show the children how to use authoring software to create a multimedia presentation, with each child presenting their arguments on screen. Begin the presentation with a picture of the ark and different animals looking out of the windows, or with pictures of the animals arranged around the ark. Give the title screen some accompanying music, and use the voice of Noah to pose the question.

By clicking on a picture of the elephant, for example, the user would be taken to a larger picture of the elephant and

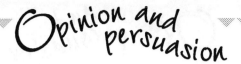

the reasons why it should be saved. Let children add their own pictures, drawn using an art package or taken from clip-art collections. They could even add musical accompaniments, in the style of *Carnival of Animals* by Saint-Saëns, or add their own voices recorded through the computer.

Display ideas
Make a wall display of Noah's ark. Display pictures of animals, perhaps using the animal cards, and include any written work completed in the activity. A display of the children's poems, defending the more unpopular animals, can be very effective.

Other aspects of the English PoS covered
Reading – 1b.
Writing – 1a, b; 2b.

Reference to photocopiable sheet
Photocopiable page 135 is a sheet provided for the purposes of summative assessment.

I'M A SPACEMAN

To develop confidence in persuasive speech.
†† *Individual speaking to the class.*
🕐 *A short 'filler' or a more substantial exercise with a number of children.*

Key background information
In this activity children are asked to try to convince the class, as persuasively as possible, that they are something they are not, such as an astronaut, a bank robber, an Olympic runner, a great artist, a sports star, a long-distance lorry driver, a scientist, a teacher. The activity develops skills of improvisation, 'thinking on one's feet', in an entertaining way. Jobs such as a police officer, lollipop person or caretaker could be used, with the activity being linked to a 'People who help us' topic for younger children.

Resources needed
Reference materials which provide information on various jobs (if required); chalkboard; writing materials.

What to do
Explain the activity to the class. Tell the children that they are going to try to convince the class that they have a 'secret identity'. Give examples such as those mentioned in 'Key background information'. Ask the children to imagine that they have a new identity. Explain that they will need to prepare a short talk – one or two minutes – describing their new identity. If the children find this difficult, allow longer for the preparation stage and provide reference materials for note-making. Allow children to choose the identities for themselves

(if they need help, you could offer suggestions). If appropriate, provide a model by being someone unlikely yourself – an alien explorer in disguise, for example. The following points might be helpful, and can be written on the board:
▲ what you have to do in your job;
▲ the good points about the job;
▲ the bad points about the job;
▲ the funniest/most interesting/most dangerous thing that has happened in the job.

Allow a few minutes for the class to fire questions at the speaker. Emphasise that the objective for the speaker is to be as convincing as possible, even though the class knows that the speaker does not really have this job! Make it clear to the children that when questioning speakers the object of the questioning is not to try to prove that the speakers are not what they say they are, but to find out about the job they do.

This is a good start for 'first person' writing, in which the writer describes a day in his or her life in the role of their character, either as a story or as a poem. The initial note-making can serve as a brainstorming session for this writing.

Suggestion(s) for extension
Very confident children may be happy to assume an identity without preparation time.

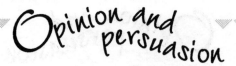

Suggestion(s) for support

This is an exercise for the most confident. For those children needing support work, another approach to the activity would be to ask the children to work in groups and assume a group identity – a group of bank robbers, part of a football team and so on. In this way the presentation can be shared.

Assessment opportunities

This activity tests confidence in the speaker, and an ability to be truly convincing. Look also for clever questioning from the audience.

Display ideas

Any written work can be made into a book. You might use a title such as 'Secret identities of class X'.

Other aspects of the English PoS covered

Writing – 1a, b, c; 2b.
Reading – 1b; 2c.

TALKING ABOUT FEELINGS

To develop confidence in dealing with feelings and emotions.

†† *Groups of three to five. Discussion leading to storytelling and then individual writing.*

🕐 *30 minutes, plus writing time.*

Key background information

This activity encourages children to discuss their own feelings and emotions. It is, of course, a sensitive area and should be approached with awareness of the differing situations of individual children. The topics suggested need not involve children discussing their own home circumstances unless they wish to.

Resources needed

Chalkboard; writing materials. For the support activity – word bank of 'emotion' vocabulary.

What to do

Place the class in groups and introduce the topics below, writing them on the board (add any further ideas that occur to you, or brainstorm possibilities with the class):
▲ a time when you felt on your own, such as a first day at a new school;
▲ a time when you felt really angry with someone;
▲ a time when you felt guilty about something you had done;
▲ a time when you couldn't stop laughing;
▲ a time when you felt very silly;
▲ a time when you were treated unfairly;
▲ a time when someone let you down.

Ask each child to choose one topic and spend a few minutes making notes about it. Stress that the important aspect is how they felt. It does not matter if more than one child in each group chooses the same topic. Ask the children to take it in turns to tell their stories to each other, working in their groups. Encourage them to include detail – how they felt; how other people felt; what they did; how it was resolved.

The accounts can be developed into autobiographical writing, either in prose or poetry. Such writing always benefits from a storytelling session first, as it enables children to put their thoughts into order and think about their whole experience.

Suggestion(s) for extension

Ask the most confident children to tell their stories to the whole class. Encourage them to be as frank as possible about their feelings.

Suggestion(s) for support

Adopting a question and answer approach for this activity will help less confident children to tell their stories. Some children will insist that they cannot think of a situation to talk about with their group. This is usually a sign of a lack of confidence rather than an inability to think of an idea. These children can be prompted and offered suggestions, but given time, such children are more likely to gain confidence by listening to others telling stories than by being forced into a situation in which they are not at ease.

Some 'emotion' vocabulary might help – annoyed, embarrassed, guilty conscience, lonely and so on.

Assessment opportunities

It is difficult to assess the speaking of individuals when they are working in groups. Cassette recorders can be used, but this is cumbersome, and listening to tapes is a time-consuming exercise. Try to visit each group in turn during the storytelling, looking for children who are able to 'hold' an audience with their storytelling.

Display/performance ideas

Stories can be recorded on tape in a radio programme format which can be played to other classes. Stories and poems can be displayed under the headings you wrote on the board.

Other aspects of the English PoS covered

Writing – 1a, b, c; 2b.

JUNK PHONE CALL

To develop confidence in persuasive speech.
♯♯ *Class discussion followed by pair brainstorming; then speaking in pairs, with the class as audience.*
🕒 *45 minutes.*

Key background information

This activity involves the use of persuasive language, without the use of body language. It is based on 'cold calling' or 'junk phone calls', frequently received by householders in the early evening, selling anything from crates of wine to the bank loans to pay for them.

Resources needed

Two telephones (or telephone substitutes such as bananas); a screen to divide the two participants; writing materials.

What to do

Initiate the activity with a class discussion on 'junk calls'. Some children will not be aware of these; their family may have no phone or may be ex-directory. Do not be totally negative in your comments – some children may have parents or older brothers and sisters who are involved in this work. Ask about the things which are usually sold in this way: double glazing, fitted kitchens, time-share holidays and so on. Talk about the reactions of the adults in the family to such telephone calls, and their strategies for dealing with them.

Next, ask the children, working in pairs, to think up a more unusual item to be sold via a junk phone call – a pet dragon, a ticket to Mars, a year's supply of tinned slugs, a wonderful magic potion. Ask them to plan out and script their phone call. They will need to think of an effective opening gambit to prevent the recipient slamming down the phone, and they will also need to consider effective responses to the comments and questions likely to be asked.

One of the pairs should now 'telephone' a member of the class, who will, of course, not know what he or she is about to be offered. This activity should take place on either side of a screen so that the performers cannot see each other. Encourage the recipient of the call to 'play along' to allow the caller to work through all the prepared ideas. In the end, the person called will have to decide whether to take up the offer, perhaps asking for further details or asking specific questions about the product.

Suggestion(s) for extension

The most confident children can be challenged by being paired with other confident children who can be asked to be particularly 'difficult' customers; ones who are aggressive, for example, or pretend not to understand what they are being told.

Suggestion(s) for support

Working in pairs allows the less confident children to contribute without necessarily having to perform. Of course, the more unscrupulous cold callers do prey on less confident people, so try to involve these children as both callers and receivers. If necessary, provide a model by taking or making some of the calls yourself, supporting less confident children.

Assessment opportunities

Look at the children's abilities to play up to each other and to create an amusing performance, as well as their attempts to persuade.

Performance ideas

Preserve the best of the telephone calls on tape.

Other aspects of the English PoS covered

Writing 1a, b, c; 2b.

SPEAKING AND
LISTENING

WHAT I LIKE

To explain why a poem, a story, a piece of music or a picture is liked.

†† *Individual.*

🕐 *10 minutes preparation time plus speaking time – a minute or two per child – and time to listen to a piece of music or a poem.*

Key background information

In this activity individuals are asked to explain what they like about a poem, story, picture or piece of music. This is not always an easy thing to do, even for adults, particularly with abstract art forms such as music. A poem often provides more material to talk about, particularly for those who are not so confident. Some preparation is beneficial. The teacher can provide a model by talking about his or her own favourite poem/picture/piece of music. The activity does not include stories or novels, as children will tend to relate the storyline rather than what it is that they like about the book. Music or art presentations can form part of the work done in art and music.

Preparation

If children are to bring things in from home – tapes, CDs, copies of pictures – this will have to be organised in advance. It is important that the audience hear or see the items themselves.

Resources needed

Copies of favourite poems and pictures; tapes of musical items; writing materials. For the support activity – word bank.

What to do

Give an overview of the activity through class discussion, and ensure that resources are available (see 'Preparation'). Suggest the following starter ideas for the talks:

▲ any background information about the piece or the writer/composer/artist;

▲ how it makes me feel and why;

▲ what it makes me think about;

▲ which are my 'favourite parts' and why;

▲ any memories it brings back.

Allow sufficient time for preparation before the presentations. Alternatively, make this an informal, 'off the cuff' exercise. Both are valuable as they demand different skills.

Allow time for question and comment by other children in the class.

Suggestion(s) for extension

A far more challenging activity is for the children to present a picture, poem or piece of music that they do not like, and explain why.

Suggestion(s) for support

This is not an easy activity. Do not expect extended talks, except from the most confident. The main difficulty children will have is in finding an appropriate vocabulary to describe the art work and their feelings about it. Help by providing words, perhaps on the board. These may be specific words connected with each art form, such as 'rhythm', 'colour', 'rhyme'; 'emotion' words such as 'sad', 'funny', 'excited', or ideas connected with the particular art work. For the latter, you can help by prompting. Poems will need to be read out, and you may feel it is appropriate to offer to do this yourself.

Assessment opportunities

Look for examples of interesting insights and use of vocabulary that arises unprompted.

Opportunities for IT

Multimedia software can be used to make a class presentation. For example, for a presentation on the children's views on different pieces of music, there could be a very brief recording of music for each child, accompanied by three or four key ideas about why the child likes, or dislikes, the music. The title page could be a list of the children's names, or even photographs of the children. By clicking on Gavin's photo, for example, the user is taken to his page. Clicking on an ear or music note produces a brief extract of the music (ten seconds at the most) and then some text is given which explains why Gavin likes or dislikes the music. The presentation could include his own voice to state the reasons. A back arrow or another picture would then take the user back to the main page so that he or she could select another child.

The multimedia presentation can be adapted for a range of likes and dislikes (food or television programmes, for instance) the information being presented using text, pictures and sounds.

Display ideas
Favourite pictures and poems and the titles of favourite pieces of music can be displayed, along with writing about them.

Other aspects of the English PoS covered
Reading – 1a; 2b.
Writing – 1b.

I THINK THAT...

To build confidence in putting forward a point of view.

†† *Group discussion (groups of three to five) followed by individual speaking.*

🕐 *Up to one hour, depending on the number of groups involved, plus research time.*

Key background information
This activity asks groups to consider a contentious issue and prepare a short speech on it. In the first instance (apart from the wild-card option) the topics are 'given', but the activity can develop to allow groups and individuals to argue issues of their own.

Preparation
Photocopiable page 136 allows for up to eight groups. If necessary, manufacture more issues cards, or ask more than one group to tackle the same topic. Copy photocopiable page 136 on to card and cut out the cards.

Resources needed
Cards made from photocopiable page 136; information books relating to the various topics (optional); writing materials. For the support activity – word bank appropriate to topics.

What to do
Put the children into groups. Explain that one person in the group is to make a speech, and that the group as a whole are going to be the speech writers. (Explain that even politicians do not write their own speeches, but have people to do this.)

Give out one card to each group. The group receiving the 'wild card' will have to think up a topic of its own. (This can be done at random, or you might contrive to give this to a more able group.)

Explain that the groups are under no obligation to disapprove of what is featured on the card; they might write a speech in praise of junk food, or insist that new roads are necessary. Where possible, encourage a balanced point of view. Ask groups to consider 'both sides' of an argument.

Allow the groups sufficient time to research and to draft their speeches, and to decide who is to make them. The ideas for the speeches may come entirely from the ideas and knowledge of the children, or they can research information. This option depends on the time available. Research will add substantially to the time needed.

The speech-maker should now make the speech to the class. Following this, the class may wish to ask questions or disagree with the points of view expressed. Allow the whole group to be involved at this point as a 'panel of experts'.

This speaking and listening activity can be a useful introduction to some group project work on the issues concerned, leading to writing and display work. You may also wish to use this approach for issues which arise out of work or topics which the children are studying.

Suggestion(s) for extension
More able children can be challenged by looking at emotive language and images in the presentation of issues, and how people can be influenced by these. Newspaper advertisements for pressure groups can be a source for this. Look for the use of words such as 'rape' (of the countryside), 'slaughter', 'heartless' and so on.

Suggestion(s) for support
Some children may need support at the planning stage, particularly with vocabulary. Preparing vocabulary lists for the topics on the photocopiable sheet is a possibility. In addition, revise group planning and brainstorming with them.

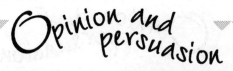

Assessment opportunities

Assess not only the quality of the speeches – forceful argument, well-organised ideas, effective presentation – but also the work of the groups. Listen to them as they prepare, and note who is contributing effectively to the discussion and who is taking on a leadership role.

Opportunities for IT

Ask the children to use a word processor to develop their ideas into a coherent and well-structured speech. They should consider how they can make the text easy to read to help them with the presentation of their speech: using a large font; using bold or italic where they should emphasise words; inserting a row of dots to indicate a pause; and perhaps inventing a code for themselves to show where they should raise their arms, laugh or gesticulate wildly!

I think that...
Cutting down forests
Killing whales
Polluting factories
Litter
Eating junk food
New roads
Animal cruelty
Wild card

Display/performance ideas

Newspaper reports on the issues raised can be displayed next to transcriptions of the speeches made. Alternatively, the speeches can be presented on tape.

Other aspects of the English PoS covered

Reading – 1b.

Writing – 1a, b, c; 2b.

Reference to photocopiable sheet

Photocopiable page 136 provides a number of pictures of controversial issues. These are used to initiate speeches and stimulate class debate. The group who receive the card with a question mark on it may decide on a topic of their own choice.

▣ SAVE OUR POND!

To develop skills in collaborative discussion and planning in groups.

†† *Groups of three to five.*

🕓 *Open-ended.*

Key background information

A local pond is to be filled in, and the land used to build an extension to a car factory. The class has decided to launch a campaign to save the pond.

This activity requires groups to work together as a team to plan a campaign, thinking about how they might involve the media and perhaps use direct action.

Preparation

To enhance the activity, find newspaper articles about environmental campaigns, or video extracts from news broadcasts of environmental issues and protests.

Resources needed

One copy per group of photocopiable page 137; newspaper cuttings; video extracts from news broadcasts of environmental issues/protests (optional); writing and drawing materials.

What to do

Spend some time talking with the children about environmental campaigns. If possible, use newspaper cuttings, and video extracts from news broadcasts. Aim for a balanced point of view in the discussion. It is all too easy to take a single-sided point of view on environmental matters, such as new road schemes.

Ask the children to work in groups. Give each group a copy of photocopiable page 137 and explain that they are going to be a committee which is organising a protest about the destruction of a pond. The section 'Getting the message across' on the photocopiable sheet lists a framework of ideas. Ask your groups to:

▲ devise a plan for fund raising;

▲ draft letters;

▲ make up effective slogans;

▲ design leaflets and posters;

▲ plan protests and 'stunts'.

A useful approach is to ask the groups to divide up the tasks, giving individuals or pairs responsibility for one aspect of the campaign. Explain that the end-product will be a display of the best materials and ideas from all the groups.

This is an open-ended activity, but point out that the situation is urgent and that the groups will need to act quickly if they are to 'save the pond'.

At the end of the group activity, assess the work and ask groups to redraft the best of what they have done for display purposes (see 'Display ideas').

SPEAKING AND LISTENING

Suggestion(s) for extension

Ensure that the most able and confident children take a leading role in the group work. This is an opportunity for them to develop their organisational skills.

Suggestion(s) for support

This is a challenging activity. A support group could work on it with a support teacher acting as 'chair'.

Assessment opportunities

Monitor the group interaction while the work is taking place. Listen for original ideas to gain attention for the campaign, and ways to raise the profile of the pond.

Opportunities for IT

The computer can be used in a number of different ways for this work.

▲ Let the children work together to produce a class newspaper or magazine about the pond. This can be done as a 'Newspaper Day' activity, with the publication produced in a single day. Divide the class into groups, with each group researching different parts of the story. Appoint an editorial board to assemble the contributions and make decisions about layout and space. It would be worthwhile to set up a class template so that the pages produced by each group have the same format and present a consistency in style. Ideally, children should use a desktop publishing package for this activity, but similar results can be achieved using word processors.

▲ Organise the children into small groups to make their own double-sided three-fold leaflet about the issues. This format gives six different columns for children to work on. A desktop publishing package can be set up, providing a format to enable children to write directly into the space provided or add their own pictures. Another possibility is for children to use an art package to create a poster about the need to save the pond.

▲ Create a multimedia presentation using an authoring package. If possible, link the various ideas on screen by incorporating sounds and moving pictures to create an interactive presentation about the issue.

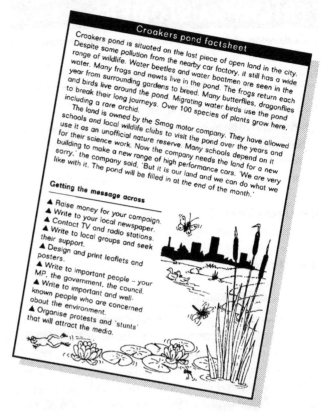

Croakers pond factsheet

Croakers pond is situated on the last piece of open land in the city. Despite some pollution from the nearby car factory, it still has a wide range of wildlife. Water beetles and water boatmen are seen in the water. Many frogs and newts live in the pond. The frogs return each year from surrounding gardens to breed. Many butterflies, dragonflies and birds live around the pond. Migrating water birds use the pond to break their long journeys. Over 100 species of plants grow here, including a rare orchid.

The land is owned by the Smog motor company. They have allowed schools and local wildlife clubs to visit the pond over the years and use it as an unofficial nature reserve. Many schools depend on it for their science work. Now the company needs the land for a new building to make a new range of high performance cars. 'We are very sorry.' the company said, 'But it is our land and we can do what we like with it. The pond will be filled in at the end of the month.'

Getting the message across

▲ Raise money for your campaign.
▲ Write to your local newspaper.
▲ Contact TV and radio stations.
▲ Write to local groups and seek their support.
▲ Design and print leaflets and posters.
▲ Write to important people – your MP, the government, the council.
▲ Write to important and well-known people who are concerned about the environment.
▲ Organise protests and 'stunts' that will attract the media.

Display ideas

Mount a 'Save our pond' display, featuring an enlarged picture of the pond on photocopiable page 137 (or other pond pictures) and a selection of letters, posters, leaflets and protest ideas created in the main activity.

Other aspects of the English PoS covered

Reading – 1b; 2c.
Writing – 1a, b, c; 2a, b.

Reference to photocopiable sheet

Photocopiable page 137 has three purposes: it is a factsheet about Croakers pond; it gives a framework for the children to use when 'getting the message across'; and it provides a picture of a pond which can be enlarged for use in a display.

SPEAKING AND LISTENING

TRICKY CUSTOMERS

To develop skills to deal with persuasive language.

†† *Pairs.*

🕐 *Three 40-minute drama sessions.*

Key background information

Children should be aware of sales techniques, particularly 'hard selling', and how to complain. This drama work addresses these two areas in a light-hearted way. It can be used to follow up work carried out in the activity 'Junk phone call' (page 73).

Resources needed

One copy per child of photocopiable page 138.

What to do

Session One

Spend a few minutes discussing 'hard selling' and ask the children to relate any examples of it that they have met, or experiences their parents may have had. It is worth introducing the topic in advance so that they can ask their parents about their experiences. Now ask the children, in pairs, to work through the drama script 'The super salesman' on photocopiable page 138. They should take a part each and read it aloud. Choose one pair to perform their version to the class. Now ask them to prepare an improvisation on what happened in the missing ten minutes. They should be allowed time to discuss this and try out ideas. Each pair should now perform their improvisation in turn.

Session Two

This builds on the work done in Session One, which should be briefly reprised, perhaps by hearing again one or two of the improvisations. Divide the class into pairs once again. Ask the pairs to work together to invent a wonderful new product which they wish to sell, either in their shop or door-to-door. Suggest new household appliances, a delicious new food, a wonderful cleaning product. The children's task is to devise a sales 'patter' (introduce this word) to convince would-be customers to buy the product.

Rearrange the pairs so that each child has a new partner. Ask each new pair to take it in turns to try to sell the product they have invented to their new partner.

Session Three

This session allows the customer to fight back by complaining. Discuss with the class what they would do if they had a complaint. Ask them for any examples of a time when they or their parents have had to complain.

Pair the children. Ask them to decide on a product they have bought which is faulty in some way – it won't work, it is of poor quality, or, like the famous parrot, it has died! Ask them to prepare their case prior to returning the goods to the shop.

Then rearrange the pairs. Ask the new pairs to take it in turns to be a complaining customer and a difficult sales person who does not want to give the money back!

The super salesman

SALESMAN Good morning, madam. I am working in the area introducing a wonderful range of new brushes that will help you do your housework in half the time...

LADY AT THE DOOR I don't need any brushes, thank you.

SALESMAN I'm sure you have plenty of ordinary brushes. But I'm sure you haven't got anything like the brushes I have here in my case! These are brand new from America and can change your life...

LADY AT THE DOOR Look, I've told you. I don't want to buy any brushes.

SALESMAN Buy? Who said anything about buy? I'm not here to sell you anything. I am just demonstrating these wonderful new inventions, as a special service to you! All I want from you, madam, is five minutes of your valuable time...

LADY AT THE DOOR I'm busy.

SALESMAN ...and in exchange for that you will receive a valuable free gift, yours to keep with no obligation! What have you got to lose?

LADY AT THE DOOR What valuable free gift?

SALESMAN Well, now, they are at the bottom of my case. Just let me come in and give you a quick demonstration...

[Ten minutes later.]

SALESMAN Well, that will be twenty-six pounds altogether!

LADY AT THE DOOR What about my free gift?

SALESMAN Oh yes! Here you are. A free full-colour sixty-page catalogue of further bargains from our wonderful range. All available on special credit terms!

Suggestion(s) for extension

This is a challenging activity for even the most confident children. Starting the performances with a pair you know to have good performance skills will act as an incentive and a model to others.

Suggestion(s) for support

Children who find drama work difficult can work with a support teacher for the paired performance. The adult can support by 'feeding' the child with lines.

Assessment opportunities

This activity provides a useful means for assessing the growth of confidence in children, and their ability to 'think on their feet'.

Opportunities for IT

Using a word processor to help them to draft the sales patter required by a sales representative, explain that the children should include instructions in their text which give the sales representative helpful hints to make his or her sales patter successful (for example, bold for words which are to be emphasised, and a set of dots for necessary pauses). Encourage the children to carry the work further to write a full script between the sales representative and an awkward customer.

Performance ideas

Successful improvisations can be taped, and developed further, perhaps by scripting.

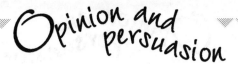

Reference to photocopiable sheet

Photocopiable page 138 provides a brief script on the topic of 'hard selling'. The middle section, in which the 'victim' agrees to buy something, has been left out and is improvised in the activity by the children.

NO THANK YOU

To learn how not to be persuaded.

†† *Whole class, then groups of three.*

🕐 *40 minutes.*

Key background information

Children all too often find themselves in trouble because they are unable to say no to those older or stronger than themselves, whether they be adults or other children. Such incidents are rarely as serious as actual abduction, of course. It is important to ensure that children are informed of dangers, and rules that attempt to deal with them. Most schools, for example, have clear rules about what to do if children are not met at the end of the school day (usually return to the classroom and wait) or if someone unfamiliar approaches them to take them home. Children and parents must be made fully aware of these rules. They will be particularly effective if the children have been involved in drawing them up, and the final discussion activity is designed to do this.

It is important in the discussion and follow-up work that the dangers from adults should not be overemphasised. Cases of child abuse by strangers are very rare and children should not regard the world as a place where menace lurks round every corner and no adult can be trusted. Children are far more likely to be placed in difficult situations by their own peers, and the short script 'Joining the gang' reflects this.

If the teacher feels it is appropriate, the work can be extended to include discussion on drug and solvent abuse. This activity may be best carried out during a drama session.

Resources needed

Copies of photocopiable page 139 (one between three is sufficient); chalkboard. For the extension activity – writing materials.

What to do

Introduce the topic with a class discussion on when it is important to say no. The poem 'Eddy Scott goes out to play' can be used here, but use this with caution, as children in the class may be in a similar position to Eddy.

Outside, the street is dark with rain,
The arcade is brightly lit with screens;
Eddy feeds his dinner money
To hypnotising fruit machines.

'Don't get into trouble.
Don't talk to funny men,
Here's a pound to buy your dinner.'
Eddy's left alone again.

The coins clunk down, the fruit rolls round
The bright lights flash like mad,
Then disappear like the dinner
Eddy hasn't had.

Eddy's mum's at work all day,
Eddy's dad has gone away.
Hot or cold, wet or fine,
Eddy Scott's sent out to play.

The money's gone. No food to eat.
Eddy checks round all the trays
In case somebody's missed a coin.
'No money, sonny?' someone says.

'Don't get into trouble,
Don't talk to funny men,
Here's a pound to buy your dinner.'
Eddy's left alone again.

'I'll lend you money if you like,
Or how about some sweets?
I've seen you here and there before
Wandering round the streets.'

Eddy's mum's at work all day,
Eddy's dad has gone away.
Hot or cold, wet or fine,
Eddy Scott's sent out to play.

'Would you like a slap-up meal?
You would? Get in the car,
I'll take you to a place I know
That isn't very far.'

'Don't get into trouble,
Don't talk to funny men,
Here's a pound to buy your dinner.'
Eddy's left alone again.

Mum gets home at six o'clock,
'Eddy, are you home?' she'll call.
There'll be no answer: just her voice
Echoing along the hall.

Eddy's mum's at work all day,
Eddy's dad has gone away.
Hot or cold, wet or fine,
Eddy was sent out to play.

by David Orme

SPEAKING AND LISTENING

Write a list of situations on the board. These might include:

▲ dealing with an approach by an unknown or little-known adult;

▲ dealing with a known adult – family member or friend of the family – behaving in an unacceptable way;

▲ dealing with peer pressure to do something the child doesn't want to do, or which the child knows is wrong.

Give out copies of the short open-ended script 'Joining the gang' on photocopiable page 139. Read it through with the class, then divide the children into threes. If required, the names can be changed to reflect the gender balance of the groups. 'Chris' can be a boy or girl. Ask half the class to imagine that Chris says no to the situation, and the other half to assume that he or she says yes. Ask them to improvise the outcomes and present their ideas to the class.

As a class, discuss the various outcomes, and the best way for Chris to get out of the difficult situation he or she is in. This can be opened up to include the other situations on your list on the board.

Extend the improvisation work, basing the work on a different situation, and perhaps in a further drama session, by using the lines below. Ask the groups to include one of them in their improvisation.

▲ 'Your Mum asked me to give you a lift home.'

▲ 'Let's go and get him.'

▲ 'Go on, try one – unless you're scared.'

▲ 'It's easy. Just put it in your pocket when she's not looking.'

Suggestion(s) for extension

More able children can perform a 'scribing' function during the class discussion. They could follow this up by producing a list of 'Say No' rules, to be displayed in the classroom.

Suggestion(s) for support

If children are not confident in improvisation and performance, a support teacher can help by coaching groups requiring support or even appearing as a character.

Assessment opportunities

This activity can be used to assess group work, and confidence in speaking and performing. What is most important is that the children learn and remember the lessons implicit in the work. Return to the topic after a week, and see how well they have remembered the 'rules' devised.

Opportunities for IT

The 'Say No' rules created in the extension activity can be written up using a word processor, art or drawing package.

Display/performance ideas

Any of the drama work done can be developed by scripting or further improvisation to make a polished performance, perhaps for an assembly.

Display the 'Say No' rules (which have been produced in the extension activity and 'Opportunities for IT') in the classroom.

Joining the gang

JOE It's easy! Just look around the shop to find something she's run out of. Ask her for that so she has to go into the back of the shop. Then take the sweets and put them in your pocket. Just take one of each so that she doesn't notice they're missing.

CHRIS What if I get caught?

SAMANTHA You won't get caught!

JOE You've got to do it. Otherwise you can't be in the gang. It's a test. We've all done it.

SAMANTHA If you don't do it, it proves you're a chicken. We don't have chickens in our gang!

JOE *[acts like a chicken]* Cluck, cluck, cluck!

SAMANTHA Go on, do it now. If you don't we'll tell the whole class you're just a baby!

JOE A baby chicken! Cluck cluck!

Other aspects of the English PoS covered

Writing – 1b, c; 2b.

Reference to photocopiable sheet

Photocopiable page 139 contains the text of the 'starter' script 'Joining the gang'. It should be continued through improvisation, followed by a class discussion on the possible outcomes of the situation.

Storytelling and performance

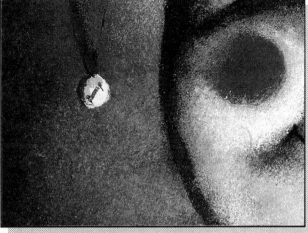

This chapter develops skills of narrative discourse, and links them to performance through drama activities. A book of this nature, with a broad overview of speaking and listening, cannot cover all the possibilities for drama work. The activities do, however, offer some fundamentals of both improvised and scripted drama, and many of them suggest drama-related work as an outcome or as part of the process of the activity.

Speaking in public can be traumatic for less confident children. The work in this chapter suggests a range of performing strategies to develop confidence – in reading aloud a story or poem, performing from a script, extemporising from a set of notes or speaking 'off the cuff'. Apart from the latter, a confident performance relies on preparation, whether this involves 'talking through' work to be performed, rehearsal or learning by heart.

Storytelling is an excellent way of writing stories, both fictional and 'true accounts'. All teachers will know children who are able to tell stories, real or imaginary, in a fluent and entertaining way, but who become stilted and dull when they try to commit their ideas to paper. Storytelling can be seen as a 'brainstorming' process in which the story develops and in which essential changes can be easily made before the story is written down. If a process other than direct writing by the storyteller – taping or scribing, for example – can follow the storytelling, there is a possibility that at least some of the liveliness and spontaneity can be retained.

SPEAKING ALOUD

To develop effective performance skills.

†† *Individual, pair or group performance of a favourite poem, leading to a 'poetry show'.*

🕒 *Open-ended.*

Key background information

This activity focuses on the performance of a poem. Poetry is ideal for performance as it is short, often rhythmical and frequently designed for performance. If the children are allowed to choose their own poems for reading, this should be monitored by the teacher. A poetry performance should have a range of moods, with poems that are both funny and serious. Children are often most likely to choose funny poems, which can limit the performance possibilities.

Preparation

For this activity the children will need a poem that they feel comfortable and confident with, whether it is written by themselves, a classmate or an adult poet.

Resources needed

A range of poems for performance (see 'Preparation'). Provide poetry collections which the children can choose poems from if they are not using poems written by themselves.

What to do

The performers and the audience are sold short if the performance is not thoroughly prepared. The first task in this activity is for the reader to know the poem thoroughly. Spend a little time talking about the poem with each child, pair or group. If the poem describes a character, ask the performer what he or she thinks about the character. If it is a sad poem, talk about the sad things that happen to everyone from time to time and how we feel about them. If it is a funny

poem, ask about similar funny things that might have happened to the reader. This 'talking round' the poem may seem peripheral to the performance; it is in fact central to it.

Once the understanding process has taken place, children are ready to start work on their performance. Learning by heart is one option, though it is generally best to allow children to have a copy with them during a performance, as nervousness and the effort of recall can seriously affect the presentation. Listen to an initial reading and give help with pronunciation and making sense of the lines through awareness of stress and punctuation.

Suggestion(s) for extension

Confident children can be given more challenging texts, such as pre-twentieth century poems.

Suggestion(s) for support

Children can increase their confidence by performing as part of a group or 'chorus'. Aim for variety; a poem can be broken up, with some sections being read by individuals and other parts read by pairs or groups.

Assessment opportunities

In assessing young performers, look for all the points noted above. Above all, look for a sense of enjoyment in the reading of the poem. Observe the audience. If they are enjoying the reading, the performer has learned a great deal about performance skills.

Performance ideas

After careful rehearsal (though not too much, as there is a danger that freshness can disappear), present your 'poetry show' to the school, another class or parents. An enjoyable project is to prepare a performance especially for infants, and then perform it to the younger classes or the local infant school. Children will generally rise to the occasion and will have a great sense of satisfaction about what they have achieved.

Other aspects of the English PoS covered

Reading – 1a, d; 2a.

📢 LISTENING TO A STORY

To encourage careful listening to a story.

†† *Whole class, then individual.*

🕒 *15-minute assessment following a listening session. Note: This is a suggested time only – the assessment should not be a 'timed' activity.*

Key background information

In encouraging attentive listening it is vital to ensure that the story chosen is appropriate to the interests of the class, and that it is told in an interesting and effective way. Listening

SPEAKING AND
LISTENING

to a story should be a relaxed and enjoyable activity. The knowledge that a task is to be a consequence can be threatening and may spoil the enjoyment. Assessment activities should therefore be occasional, limited and enjoyable.

Preparation
Choose and prepare a story to read to the children. Ensure that the story is suitably challenging.

Resources needed
A story; one copy per child of photocopiable page 140; writing materials; photocopiable assessment page 149 (as required).

What to do
Settle the class in the story corner. Read the children a short story of your choice, ensuring that you mention the title and author of the story two or three times. Maintain the children's attention by pausing occasionally and asking them to predict what happens next, or what the final outcome of the tale will be. When you have finished the story ask each child to complete the questionnaire on a copy of photocopiable page 140. You can choose whether or not to warn them in advance that there will be 'quiz questions' to be answered. (It is interesting to see whether the response to the activity is different.)

Suggestion(s) for extension
A more challenging activity is to use the story as a basis for creative writing. This might involve continuing the story or using a favourite character in a new story.

Suggestion(s) for support
During the reading, make full use of any pictures to support understanding of the narrative with visual clues.

For assessment purposes, those who find writing difficult can answer the questions verbally, perhaps with a support teacher writing down the answers. Pairing children is another possibility.

Assessment opportunities
The activity offers a means of summative assessment and a photocopiable sheet is provided for this purpose. Watch the children as they listen to the story. (This is easier if someone other than yourself reads the story.) Observing the children gives a good guide as to who is involved, and who is not, although sometimes, apparently inattentive children can be absorbing the story, while apparently attentive ones are actually in a dream! The questionnaire allows you to judge how much has been absorbed, although the writing activity can hamper recall.

Other aspects of the English PoS covered
Reading – 1a, c, d.
Writing – 1b.

Reference to photocopiable sheets
Photocopiable page 140 offers a series of questions children can answer after almost any story, either filling in the sheet themselves or giving the answers verbally, with a helper scribing. Photocopiable page 149 is a sheet provided for the purposes of summative assessment.

GOSSIP

To build confidence in telling stories.
†† *Whole class, then groups.*
🕐 *40 minutes.*

Key background information

Generally, people are naturally good storytellers. We recount incidents in our own lives, often amusing ones, to our family and colleagues. The incidents and events themselves are often quite trivial – a traffic hold-up, a minor domestic crisis, an amusing gaffe by someone in authority. Everyone likes to gossip! Despite the triviality of gossip, we use all our skills of timing, exaggeration and body language to entertain our listeners.

For children, problems arise when a true incident has to be produced as a written narrative. The language all too often becomes stilted and tedious. No attempt is made to gain the attention of an audience, with an exciting opening and, of course, the body language and timing is not available.

This activity seeks to capitalise on natural storytelling skills by asking children, in groups, to tell each other stories about real incidents and events. The stories told can be used as the raw material for various forms of writing.

Resources needed

A cassette recorder for each group, if possible; writing materials.

What to do

This activity requires substantial introductory discussion if the children are going to be successful. Simply inviting them to tell stories will not be very productive. The best lead into the activity is for you to talk about your own funny experiences: the day I forgot my key and couldn't get into the house; the day the dog escaped; the day I found I had forgotten my money when I got to the checkout. Include in your telling how you felt, and what the people involved said. Ask one of the more confident children to recount a story, prompting him or her by asking questions such as 'What did you think? What did they say? What happened next?'

Now put the children into groups and ask them to take it in turns to tell stories, using a cassette recorder. Encourage the other group members to ask questions as the narrative proceeds.

The recordings can be used as the raw material for writing. Suggest that the children transcribe the stories. This will provide the freshness and liveliness that stories written directly on to paper may lack.

Suggestion(s) for extension

The most confident children can be asked to tell their stories to the whole class.

Suggestion(s) for support

Many children will not have the confidence to tell a story of their own, but can be helped if you or a support teacher develop the story with them.

Assessment opportunities

Listening in to the groups will enable you to assess the confidence of individual storytelling. A good guide to the success of this can be heard in the laughter of the other members of the group, as the stories will often be amusing.

Display ideas

The final written stories can be displayed. It is particularly interesting to link the written stories with tapes of the initial storytelling sessions.

Other aspects of the English PoS covered

Writing – 1b, c; 2b.

WHOSE SHOES?

To develop imaginative speculation and inference from limited evidence.

†† *Whole class, followed by group conference/report back. (Groups of three to five.)*

🕐 *15–20 minutes, plus the report-back stage.*

Previous skills/knowledge needed

It would be helpful if the children have carried out work on people, which includes the reading of poems and stories, prior to this activity. This would take the form of discussion of the various characters who have been presented in the poems and stories. 'Who owns what?' (page 55) and 'Being a detective' (page 51) would be useful activities to precede this one.

Key background information

This activity requires children to develop descriptions of characters through group discussion. It is a valuable exercise in the development of storytelling and story writing.

Resources needed

One copy per group of photocopiable page 141; writing materials.

What to do

Give each group a copy of photocopiable page 141. Explain to the children that the task of each group is to build up an imaginative description of the owner of one of the shoes. (You might suggest that the shoes are clues in a police 'missing person' inquiry.) With the class, work through one of the shoes as a model, reinforcing the important elements of character: appearance, occupation, the 'type' of person he or she might be. Ask questions, such as 'What do other people think of the character? What does the character most enjoy doing? Does the character have a family, or pets? What job does the character have?' Finally, ask the children to name the character and think of a short story to explain how he or she lost the shoe.

Ask the children to repeat the activity in their groups. You may either allow the groups to decide on which shoe they will work on, or you can allocate the different types. Give them ten to fifteen minutes to prepare a report on 'whose shoes'. If the children are unfamiliar with group conferencing, they will need extra support including an explanation of the roles of the chair and the scribe. Emphasise the importance of taking turns and careful listening. The report should be presented by the whole group, each child taking responsibility for one particular area – appearance, type of person, job, family and so on.

Following the group-speaking activity, other groups can demonstrate how well they have listened by asking questions about the character who has been created.

Suggestion(s) for extension

A particularly confident group could be given a 'blank card' and asked to design their own shoes before speculating on the owner. These can be fantasy based – an alien's shoes, a ghost's shoes, a giant's shoes.

Suggestion(s) for support

A support group may carry out the activity with a teaching assistant or support teacher encouraging the discussion with leading questions, and acting as scribe.

Assessment opportunities

The final presentation provides an opportunity to listen to each child, and to assess how well the group conference has worked. A particular group can be taped so that individual contributions can be assessed later. It is important that all children in a group should contribute and interact effectively.

Opportunities for IT

Show the children how to use an authoring package to make a multimedia presentation which is based on a pair of shoes which belong to a character. If the title screen presents each pair of shoes, the user can then click on a particular pair to be taken to the section that is based on that pair of shoes. Footprints could take users back to the main menu again. Produce the presentation so that each group creates a set of linked screens which show different components of the person's character: occupation, appearance and so on. The screens could contain pictures, text and even spoken words which have been recorded using a microphone connected to the computer.

A more ambitious project is to make an interactive multimedia presentation, giving children multiple-choice options for each aspect of the character, so that the user can build up a view of the person, from the shoes up. It could even include pictures which fit together to form a picture of the person.

SPEAKING AND
LISTENING

Display ideas

The activity can 'come alive' if it is repeated with real objects – items of clothing, personal possessions and so on. These objects can form the basis for an interesting display, with the imaginative writing displayed next to them.

Other aspects of the English PoS covered

Writing – 1c; 2b.

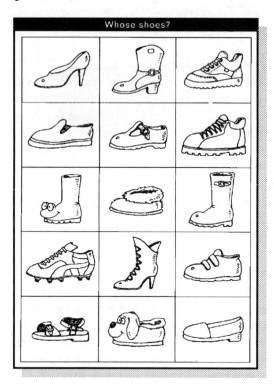

Whose shoes?

Reference to photocopiable sheet

Photocopiable page 141 shows a range of various types of shoes. Each group must choose one shoe and prepare a report, for presentation to the class, on the character who might own such shoes.

⬛ PREPARED STORIES

To build confidence in storytelling.

†† *Individual.*

🕐 *20 minutes preparation, plus a few minutes for each performance.*

Previous skills/knowledge needed

This activity requires storytelling skills. It would be a good follow-up exercise to the activity 'Gossip' (page 84).

Key background information

Telling a story to the whole class is more daunting than to a partner or small group. This activity supports children by encouraging them to use notes for their storytelling. (The activity 'Speaking aloud', on page 82 gives advice on supporting children speaking in public.)

Resources needed

Chalkboard; cassette recorders; writing materials.

What to do

Explain to the class that you would like them to prepare a story of an event that really happened to them. Ask the children to make a set of notes, listing main points in their true story. It will help if you provide a model by listing half a dozen quick notes about a story of your own on the board. Stress the need for an overview (This is about a time when...), bringing the story to life by including dialogue (Then my mum said...) and providing a strong ending.

When the children have made their notes ask them to tell their stories, using their notes as 'memory aids'. Asking a particularly confident child to speak first will set the tone and provide a model for others.

Let the children expand their notes into written stories where appropriate, but this should not be seen as an inevitable consequence of storytelling.

Suggestion(s) for extension

Look for more structured and extended narratives from the most able children, perhaps using a question and answer session to follow the main activity.

Suggestion(s) for support

Children requiring support work may need help with the note-making, perhaps working with a more confident partner or with a support teacher. Sometimes children have difficulty in reading their own notes, especially when under pressure, and it can help to have these written out for them. Children who need a lot of assistance may find it useful to collaborate with a support teacher on a story.

Assessment opportunities

This activity is a good opportunity to hear each child speak and to evaluate their confidence, range of vocabulary, and ability to speak coherently from note cues.

Opportunities for IT

Let the children use a word processor to write, edit and organise their notes for the presentation. Encourage them to add information which will assist them with making the presentation itself: words to emphasise, or pauses to insert, actions to incorporate, and so on. If the notes are made using a large font, the children will find that they are easier to read and follow during the presentation.

Performance ideas

The children's stories could be taped to create a sound anthology.

Other aspects of the English PoS covered

Writing – 1b; 2b.

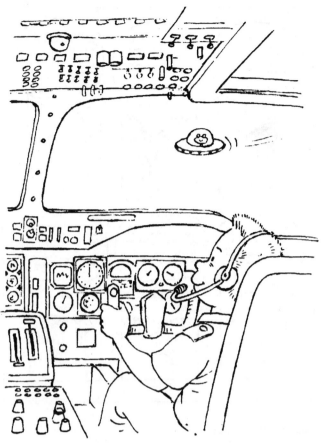

are to describe a day in their lives, using the word 'I'. Allow 20 minutes for preparation and note-making.

At this point, allocate a subject for the storytelling, offer suggestions, or leave the choice up to each child. Probably the most satisfactory approach is to allow a free choice, but have a range of suggestions ready for those who need them (see below).

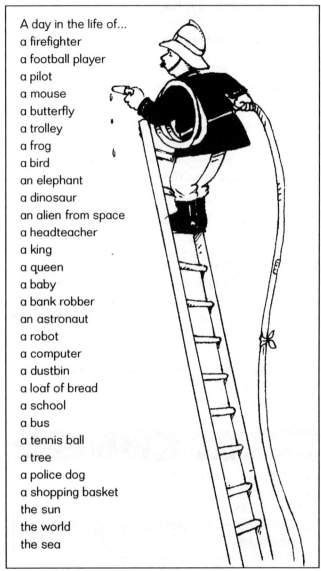

A day in the life of...
a firefighter
a football player
a pilot
a mouse
a butterfly
a trolley
a frog
a bird
an elephant
a dinosaur
an alien from space
a headteacher
a king
a queen
a baby
a bank robber
an astronaut
a robot
a computer
a dustbin
a loaf of bread
a school
a bus
a tennis ball
a tree
a police dog
a shopping basket
the sun
the world
the sea

Once the note-making has been completed, ask the children to present their accounts of 'A day in the life of...', thinking carefully about appropriate expression.

I AM A...

To build confidence in telling an amusing story, using appropriate expression.

†† Individual.

🕑 20 minutes for preparation and note-making, followed by short (five-minute) performances.

Key background information
An effective way to encourage personal involvement in a story is to tell it in the first person. In this activity the storyteller has to adopt the persona of another person, an animal or even an object. Making the story humorous helps further, as the teller will respond to the appreciative feedback from the listeners. This approach – note-making and drafting; then storytelling; followed by writing – is valuable in that it reinforces a drafting approach to writing.

Resources needed
Writing materials. For the support activity – word bank.

What to do
Explain to the children that you are going to ask them to prepare a story to tell to the class. (If they are unfamiliar with this type of activity, ask them to work initially with a partner or in a group.) Explain that, in this story, they are going to become someone or something new, and that they

Suggestion(s) for extension
This activity is appropriate for a wide range of abilities, though you will obviously expect a higher level of achievement from more confident children. Encourage such children to tackle more challenging 'lives' such as inanimate objects – the sun, the world, the sea and so on.

Suggestion(s) for support
Some children will need help at the note-making stage, particularly with vocabulary. It may be helpful to allocate a

subject to these children, along with a vocabulary list. Another possibility is to ask children to work with a partner; they could then be a pair of items. Try to avoid always asking for a written follow-up to speaking and listening work. Children requiring support can often excel in purely verbal activities, and 'writing it up' can be inhibiting.

Assessment opportunities
A range of skills can be assessed in this activity. Observe the children's note-making, storytelling, and confidence in public speaking.

Opportunities for IT
Show the children how to use handwritten or word-processed notes as the basis for a multimedia presentation using text, pictures and the child's own spoken voice which has been recorded using a microphone linked to the computer. Let the children look at some CD-ROM stories to see how they are laid out and how the pictures are used to make the story interesting, as a stimulus for the making of the multimedia presentation.

Display/performance ideas
Any written work can be displayed with appropriate pictures, perhaps using a 'giant' speech bubble for the story. Particularly amusing stories can be developed into performances, perhaps for an assembly.

Other aspects of the English PoS covered
Writing – 1b, c; 2b.

STORY STARTS

To build confidence in improvising stories.

†† *Group or class storytelling and performing in groups of three or four.*

⏱ *20 minutes storytelling, followed by group presentations.*

Previous skills/knowledge needed
Ensure children are fully confident with working on a group project. For play writing, introduce this activity by looking at 'Make a play' (page 89), although it is not essential that 'Make a play' has been carried out.

Key background information
This activity allows stories to be developed as a group activity. It is an open-ended activity with a range of strategies and outcomes.

Preparation
Reproduce photocopiable pages 142, 143 and 144 on to thin card. Cut up into individual cards.

Resources needed
A set of places, people and object cards (made from copies of photocopiable pages 142, 143 and 144) for each group; a range of real objects to supplement the cards, if required; writing materials.

What to do
Form the class into groups of three or four. Hand out a set of cards to each group. Tell the children to choose one place card, three character cards, and as many object cards as they wish. Explain that the cards are to be used to initiate a story that will be told aloud, and for preparing a script for improvisation or scripted performance. Whatever is on the cards should feature in the stories. You may decide to offer just one of the options (oral story or play) or, for older and more experienced classes, allow them to choose. The groups may develop the characters in any way they wish. For drama work, the members of the groups will have to play the characters on the cards. In this case it may be helpful to replace the pictures with a similar range of real objects which can be used as props. Some objects – the small boat, for instance – could be mimed.

Ask the groups to prepare a first draft in note form of their story/play. Each group should then outline its story idea to the class, asking for feedback and suggestions from the other children. These should be carefully noted, and decisions made within the groups on whether to include the ideas. Another approach is to present the first draft as an improvised play, explaining beforehand who the various characters are. Following this they can work on a final draft.

SPEAKING AND LISTENING

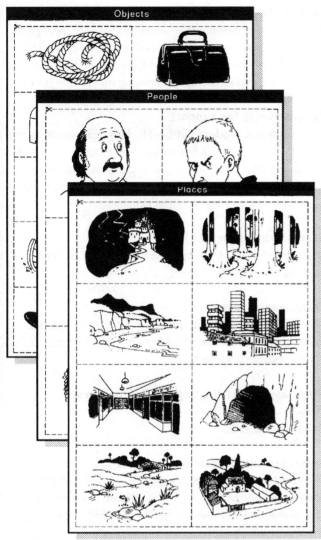

Suggestion(s) for extension

A more difficult exercise is to allocate the cards to the groups yourself, giving each group one place card, three character cards, and one or more object cards. By handing out cards which are totally unrelated to each other the activity can be made more challenging.

Suggestion(s) for support

If the children find this activity too complex, work on a class story first, scribing the ideas on the board.

Assessment opportunities

The end-product is a team effort; look particularly at how effective the children are in working as members of a team.

Opportunities for IT

Working in groups, let the children use a word processor to make the notes for their story. They can take it in turns to type in the story as the group develops it, or make use of an adult scribe. Encourage the children to redraft their story until they are satisfied that it has been improved to the best of their abilities.

Display/performance ideas

Each group's written work can be displayed alongside copies of the cards they chose for their stories. Drama work can be developed into polished performances.

Other aspects of the English PoS covered

Writing – 1b, c; 2b.

Reference to photocopiable sheets

Photocopiable pages 142, 143 and 144 are copied and cut up to make 'story start' cards to give to each group carrying out the activity. The cards are used as a stimulus for storytelling.

MAKE A PLAY

To develop drama and scripting skills.

†† *Groups of four.*

🕓 *Open-ended, but initially two 40-minute drama sessions.*

Key background information

A wide range of drama work is a vital ingredient in children's education in general and their speaking and listening work in particular. This activity offers starters in working from a script and for improvisation or script writing.

The photocopiable sheets offer the opening scenes of two adventure plays starring the same four characters. Liam is male and Geeta female, but the other two characters, Toni and Sam, can be either. Each play breaks off at a moment of crisis for the characters. The groups' task is to devise their own ending for one of the plays.

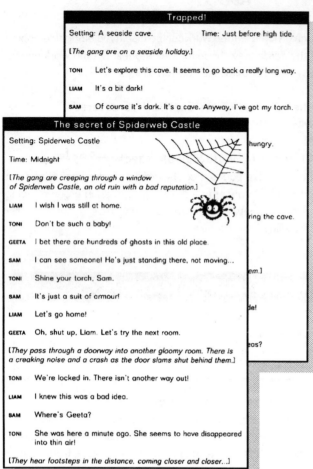

Trapped!

Setting: A seaside cave. Time: Just before high tide.

[The gang are on a seaside holiday.]

TONI Let's explore this cave. It seems to go back a really long way.

LIAM It's a bit dark!

SAM Of course it's dark. It's a cave. Anyway, I've got my torch.

The secret of Spiderweb Castle

Setting: Spiderweb Castle

Time: Midnight

[The gang are creeping through a window of Spiderweb Castle, an old ruin with a bad reputation.]

LIAM I wish I was still at home.

TONI Don't be such a baby!

GEETA I bet there are hundreds of ghosts in this old place.

SAM I can see someone! He's just standing there, not moving...

TONI Shine your torch, Sam.

SAM It's just a suit of armour!

LIAM Let's go home!

GEETA Oh, shut up, Liam. Let's try the next room.

[They pass through a doorway into another gloomy room. There is a creaking noise and a crash as the door slams shut behind them.]

TONI We're locked in. There isn't another way out!

LIAM I knew this was a bad idea.

SAM Where's Geeta?

TONI She was here a minute ago. She seems to have disappeared into thin air!

[They hear footsteps in the distance, coming closer and closer...]

Resources needed
One copy per child of photocopiable pages 145 and 146; props as required (though these can be mimed); an appropriate space in which the groups can carry out their work; writing materials.

What to do
Hand out the scripts and ask the groups to read both plays and decide which one they would like to work on. Alternatively, allocate one of the two sheets to each group.

Allow ten minutes for the children to choose parts and rehearse the scenes. Then explain that, in their groups, the children need to work out a conclusion for the plays (this can be happy or tragic). They may introduce other characters, but only if they can be played by the existing cast.

Allow half an hour for discussion, planning, and experimentation. If they wish, the groups may write down an outline script. Alternatively, they may prefer to develop their play by improvisation. Suggest these two approaches to the groups.

Finally, ask each group to perform their play, with the rest of the class as an audience. Place a time limit of, say, ten minutes on each play.

In a writing session, the groups can script the improvised part of their play more formally. Discuss with the class the conventions of script writing: for instance, the name of the character who is speaking is given before the spoken words; the stage directions are often set in italic and so on.

Suggestion(s) for extension
The groups can develop their own plot ideas for short plays, using the same characters or developing new ones. This is an excellent mixed ability activity. Those with developed writing skills might take on the scribing role for the groups.

Suggestion(s) for support
Less confident readers will benefit from having the script read through by a teacher or support teacher before the drama activity. Sight reading and performing are difficult tasks, so ensure that these children have a thorough grasp of the text before they read it aloud.

Assessment opportunities
Look specifically for performance skills, and the ability to work as a member of a team.

Performance ideas
The final versions can be performed, taped or videoed. A 'radio play' format is particularly effective, perhaps using appropriate sound effects.

Other aspects of the English PoS covered
Writing – 1a, b, c; 2b; 3a.
Reading – 1a, c; 3.

Reference to photocopiable sheets
The scripts on photocopiable pages 145 and 146 offer the opening scenes of two plays; the children choose one play and devise their own ending before performing the play for the rest of the class.

ARGUING

To develop confidence in improvising a conversation.
†† *Pairs.*
🕐 *10 minutes, then 3–5 minutes per pair.*

Key background information
This activity puts pairs of children into roles where situations of conflict develop. They have to develop a convincing dialogue, which may be serious or fantasy, in order to argue their point. The activity can be collaborative, with the children working together on the dialogue before it is presented, or confrontational, with no time to plan and the need for an immediate response.

Resources needed
Cassette recorder (optional).

What to do
Put the children into pairs, and give them a role or a situation in which two characters are in conflict. A number of suggestions are listed on the opposite page.

> **Parent and child conflicts:**
> Wanting to stay up late
> Not wanting to finish a meal
> Untidy bedrooms
> **Others:**
> Motorist and traffic warden
> Police officer and burglar
> Teacher and pupil
> Shop complaints department
> Sales representative at the door
> Two children arguing about the possession of one item
> Two students arguing over which is the best subject
> A dog and a cat, both claiming to be the best pet.

Give the children five minutes to decide and prepare on the basic elements of their performances. One possibility is to work through the activity twice, with different characters for each pair. One performance would use the collaborative model involving preparation, and the other the confrontational one suggested in 'Key background information', with the situation given to the participants for instant improvisation.

Allow each pair three to five minutes for their presentation. The pairs can then refine and develop their dialogues, perhaps for a taped performance.

Suggestion(s) for extension

With very confident children the confrontational model can be used and an instant response asked for. This sort of improvisation can be enjoyable and requires quick thinking.

Suggestion(s) for support

Choose a less challenging situation for children who are not as confident. Parent/child conflicts are familiar territory and are relatively easy to do.

Assessment opportunities

The collaborative activity is a useful means of assessing one-to-one co-operative skills. The confrontational exercise will demonstrate children's ability to 'think on their feet'.

Performance ideas

If possible, tape or video the performances.

ROUND ROBIN

To develop collaborative storytelling skills.
†† *Storytelling in groups of five or six.*
🕐 *45 minutes.*

Key background information

This activity asks children to develop a story 'off the top of their heads'. Each group is supplied with a story starter, and is asked to improvise a story, with each child taking it in turn to tell the story around the group. Children often find it difficult to get started on a story, and this is a useful way of 'brainstorming' plot and characters. To begin with, stories devised in this way are often rambling and unstructured, but this activity allows children an opportunity to reflect and revise the narratives.

Preparation

Make a set of story starters by copying photocopiable page 147 on to thin card and cutting out the pictures and text.

Resources needed

A set of story starters (made from copies of photocopiable page 147) – one card for each group; a cassette recorder for each group; writing materials.

What to do

Organise the children into groups – five or six is ideal. Provide each group with a story starter, either a picture or a first line of a story. The pictures are more challenging in that they are less specific and the children will have to invent their own first line. Discuss how the process works with the whole class. (If necessary, you could start the activity by organising a whole-class round robin, beginning the story yourself.) Stress that the purpose of the activity is not to make life difficult for the next person telling the story by creating improbable storylines that are difficult to continue (for example, by leaving the characters hanging off a cliff.)

Use a cassette recorder with each group. Ask one of the children to start telling a story based on the starter card.

SPEAKING AND LISTENING

When the first child feels that he or she has temporarily run out of ideas, the storytelling passes on to the next child in the group. The process continues round the group until the story comes to a natural conclusion.

When the story has been told, ask each group to listen to their tape and discuss how well their story went. Ask them to make notes on the good and bad aspects of the story, and discuss how it could be improved. Then ask them to record the story a second time. The stories can also be written down.

Suggestion(s) for extension
Instead of being given a story starter, children could use the same technique to tell stories that originate within their group.

Suggestion(s) for support
Children requiring extra help can work with a support teacher, who can assist each child in turn by asking questions and making suggestions. The teacher should be fully involved at the reflection/revision stage, if possible listening to the tape and making suggestions as to how it might be developed.

Assessment opportunities
The cassettes allow you to have a record of how effectively each child is participating in the group storytelling process, and how willing each child is to take a lead in developing the unfolding story and to introduce new characters.

Opportunities for IT
Transcribe the taped story on to a word processor (the children could be asked to do this) and give each of the contributors his or her own copy. Individuals, pairs or the group as a whole can then work from this original to redraft and improve the story before giving a presentation to the class.

Display/performance ideas
The stories can be presented to the class or a wider audience, either as taped presentations or 'live' performances, or as written stories.

Other aspects of the English PoS covered
Writing – 1a, b, c; 2b.

Reference to photocopiable sheet
Photocopiable page 147 provides a number of starter sentences and starter pictures. These are used as a stimulus for group storytelling.

PICTURE STORY

To build confidence in working together as a group.
†† *Groups of three or four.*
🕘 *20 minutes.*

Key background information
Photocopiable page 148 shows a series of pictures, in comic-strip style, printed in the wrong order. The object is for the groups to decide, through group discussion, on the correct order for the story, thus developing an understanding of narrative. As the ordering clues are entirely visual, this activity is suitable for children who are less confident when dealing with a sequencing exercise involving text.

Resources needed
One copy per group of photocopiable page 148; sheets of paper; scissors; glue.

What to do
Give each group a pair of scissors, glue and a copy of photocopiable page 148. Ask each group to appoint one person to cut up the sheets into individual pictures. Explain that the pictures have been printed in the wrong order on the sheet and that the children need to work together in their groups to place them in the correct order. Unless you wish to store the pictures for further use, the final order can be pasted on to a sheet of paper. When they have decided on the correct order, the children can write up the story in short paragraphs, giving each character a name and so on, writing underneath the appropriate picture. The children will need to paste their pictures on to several sheets of paper if they write up the story, in order to leave sufficient space underneath each picture to write.

Suggestion(s) for extension
Cut out the pictures in advance, then hand them out in sets, in mixed order, but retain one of the pictures. Explain the activity in the same way, but tell the children that one of the pictures is missing. Their task is to:
▲ arrange the pictures in the correct order;

▲ find where the gap is in the story;

▲ draw the picture that fills in the gap.

Their picture can then be compared with the retained missing picture. Both the main activity and the extension activity can be done 'against the clock' or even turned into a competitive race.

Suggestion(s) for support

This is a fairly straightforward task, but less confident groups may need a support teacher's involvement, guiding the group with leading questions such as 'What happens next? What do you think they might want to do in the shop?' and so on.

Assessment opportunities

The importance of the task lies in the discussion rather than the success of the outcome. Try to listen in to the discussions, noting logical reasoning and co-operative skills.

Opportunities for IT

Ask each child in the group to use a word processor to write a caption for one part of the story. Encourage the children to experiment with suitable fonts and formats to make the captions interesting in their design. Display the captions underneath the pictures of the story.

Display ideas

The pasted-up pictures can be coloured in and displayed with the written texts (either handwritten or word-processed).

Other aspects of the English PoS covered

Writing – 1c; 2b.

Reference to photocopiable sheet

Photocopiable page 148 provides a series of pictures which are in a mixed-up order. The children cut out the pictures and assemble them into a correct sequence.

RETELLING STORIES

To develop the skills required to retell a well-known story clearly and accurately.

†† *Individual storytelling to a partner, group or the class.*

🕐 *A few minutes per person.*

Previous skills/knowledge needed

The children should have a knowledge of well-known fairy stories, traditional stories and folk tales. You will need to discover what stories individual children are familiar with, and let them use the appropriate ones for the activity.

Key background information

Telling a story 'in your own words' is a complex activity. Children often attempt to relate the plot of a television programme or film, but are defeated by its sheer complexity. This activity asks them to retell a traditional story such as *Cinderella*, *Hansel and Gretel*, *Little Red Riding Hood*, or any folk story with which they are familiar. These may come from a range of cultures. These stories, for the most part, have simple, well-structured and logical plots. Modern stories may work perfectly well, if they are simple enough. It is preferable to ask the children to tell a story that appeals to them, rather than ask them to prepare one specially.

Preparation

If the children are confident enough, they can retell the story without preparation. Some children may prefer to refresh their memories by glancing through the story before telling it aloud. In this case they will need a copy of the text.

Resources needed

Copies of the children's chosen stories (see 'Preparation'), if needed.

What to do

Ask each child to choose a story, and explain that the children will be telling a story to their classmates. They may need prompting with suggestions here. Explain why you are not asking them to retell *Star Wars* or *The Lord of the Rings* – the story must be simple, and possible to retell in under five minutes.

Decide on how you wish to organise the storytelling. Pair work is appropriate for the least confident, but it does make monitoring difficult. Telling a story to the whole class requires confidence and gives opportunities for assessment, but it is time-consuming if all the children are to be involved. Group work, with each group member taking it in turn to tell a story, is a useful compromise. This will also allow the same story to be used by different children, as each child telling the story of *Cinderella*, for example, can be placed in a different group. Ask the children to imagine that their partner, group or class has not heard the story before, so they must tell the complete tale. Encourage performance skills – the object of telling a story is not to send the audience to sleep!

Suggestion(s) for extension

More confident children can choose stories which have a greater complexity. Look out for effective speakers choosing an easy option and try to extend their abilities by suggesting a story which has more depth. Encourage the use of the child's own vocabulary, and allow them to 'embroider' their story with humorous additions.

Suggestion(s) for support

Children who require support will gain most by working with a partner, or support teacher, who can prompt where necessary.

Assessment opportunities

Look out for the children's ability to remember stories, to tell them in the correct sequence, and to grasp and give due emphasis to the important elements in the plot. Also note effective performance skills.

Display/performance ideas

Encourage children to develop their performances of the stories, then to retell them to a younger audience. If an infant class is available, the children could take it in turns to tell small groups of them their stories. If they do this, ask them to evaluate their own performances.

Other aspects of the English PoS covered

Reading – 1a, c.

A RECORDED STORY

To develop attentive listening to a story on an audio cassette or CD.

†† *Whole class.*

🕐 *30 minutes.*

Key background information

Listening to a story on tape robs the listener of the body language of the storyteller. Concentration is therefore that much more difficult. For this reason it is well worth varying the pattern of 'storytime' to include storytelling without visual clues. This activity is an appropriate one for summative assessment.

Preparation

Prepare a story tape in advance, if you are not using commercial materials. The story should not be longer than ten minutes. Another possibility is to provide a tape of a child reading a story. This could be done on a 'swap' basis, with one class preparing a story cassette for another class to listen to. Ensure good quality reproduction, particularly if there are hearing-impaired children in the class. Prepare a questionnaire on the text, for the children to complete after they have listened to the story. The questionnaire should

SPEAKING AND LISTENING

contain some or all of these components:

▲ memory questions on factual details in the story;

▲ names of characters and locations;

▲ details of the action, such as who did what;

▲ reasoning questions, for example questions on the motives of the characters;

▲ sequencing questions, such as 'What happened after...?'

Some questions could be answered with tick boxes, reducing the writing element. Aim for about ten minutes of questions.

Storytelling and performance	
Name:	
Class:	
Age:	
Date of assessment:	
Comments on listening skills:	
Can listen attentively to a short story told by the teacher.	
Can listen and respond to a story on tape/CD.	
Can concentrate on listening despite distractions.	
Can listen and respond to instructions effectively.	
Can understand and retell the sequence of events in a simple narrative.	
Can understand and comment on the motives of characters in a story.	
Can predict outcomes in a narrative.	
Can make deductions from evidence heard in a story.	
General comments:	

Resources needed

A cassette recorder; story tape; questionnaire (one for each child); writing materials; photocopiable assessment page 149 (as required).

What to do

Assemble the children in the 'reading corner' and play them the tape you have prepared. Before starting, explain that there will be a 'quiz' on the story to be answered once they have heard it. During the playing of the story take the opportunity to observe the class (see 'Assessment opportunities'). Once the class have heard the story, give each child a copy of the questionnaire you have prepared and ask the children to write down the answers to the questions you have set. Allow sufficient time to answer, then collect in the written responses.

Suggestion(s) for extension

The questionnaire can be differentiated for more able children with a range of more challenging questions, such as asking what question they would most like to ask one of the

characters, or how they would have resolved the problem/dilemma in the story. Allow a little extra time for children to answer the more demanding questions.

Suggestion(s) for support

For less competent readers the questionnaire can be filled in by a support teacher who will ask the questions. The objective in the activity is to assess listening rather than writing, so a spoken response is perfectly acceptable. Ensure that the questionnaire is filled in as soon as possible after the story has been heard.

Assessment opportunities

Observation during the listening. Take the opportunity to observe and note the ability of individual children to concentrate on their listening. Negative indicators are fidgeting, and misbehaving; positive indicators are responding to the story, by laughing for example.

Written response. The questionnaire will give a good guide to the quality of a child's listening. The activity can be used for summative assessment alongside, or as an alternative to, 'Listening to a story' (page 82).

This activity is appropriate for summative assessment and a photocopiable record sheet is provided for this purpose.

Performance ideas

This activity can be linked in with tape work, such as making a story tape for another class.

Reference to photocopiable sheet

Photocopiable page 149 provides a record sheet for summative assessment.

CHANGES

To develop narrative and storytelling skills by telling 'a true story'.

⭐ *Whole class, then individual.*

🕐 *3–5 minutes per child, plus preparation.*

Previous skills/knowledge needed
For this activity the children will need to have note-making skills.

Key background information
Not all children find it easy to talk about themselves. This activity, in which children are asked to reflect on the important changes in their lives, provides a focus for their thinking. The activity is a foil for some of the more light-hearted activities in this chapter.

Care is needed when dealing with children who have suffered traumatic changes in their lives, such as family breakdown or the death of a parent. The teacher is the best judge of what is appropriate for individual children, perhaps guiding them towards some of the less personal topics suggested below.

Resources needed
Chalkboard; writing materials.

What to do
Introduce the topic of change. (This is often used as a broad cross-curricular topic in junior schools, and this activity can fit in with that.) Discuss with the class as a whole some of the most important changes in their lives, and make a list of them on the board. The changes suggested will be mainly childhood ones such as:

▲ first day at playschool/infant school/junior school;

▲ a new teacher;

▲ moving house;

▲ first time away from home without parents;

▲ a new baby in the family;

▲ finding an exciting new hobby or interest.

Extend the discussion by asking what the most important changes in the life of an adult may be. (Leaving school, further education, first job, marriage, first child, changing jobs, and retirement are the more obvious ones.)

Now ask the children to work by themselves to make notes for a talk which they will give to their classmates. Ask them to decide on a change that was important to them. The list on the board will help them with this. To help the children prepare, provide them with a structure on which to base their talks and work through it with them.

An appropriate structure is:

▲ overview – what was the change?

▲ special memories of the change and how I felt about it at the time;

▲ good things about the change;

▲ bad things about the change;

▲ how I feel about the change now.

Ask them to prepare their talks in note form. When they are ready allow three to five minutes for each talk, with time for questions.

Suggestion(s) for extension
The structure given in 'What to do' could be made more complex by asking more able children to reflect on how the changes that were difficult at the time have actually been to their long-term benefit. Another, more challenging exercise is to ask them to make notes and then talk on the topic of 'How I have changed'.

Suggestion(s) for support
Less confident writers should not be held back. Ask a support teacher or scribing partner to help with the note-making.

Assessment opportunities
This is an opportunity to assess general speaking and performance skills and confidence. Perhaps more important is that the activity can help to assess the child's growing maturity and ability to look at his or her life in perspective and reflect upon it.

Display ideas
The talks can be written up for display, perhaps illustrated with photographs brought from home taken during the period the child talked about.

Other aspects of the English PoS covered
Writing – 1a, b; 2a, b.

SPEAKING AND LISTENING

Extending vocabulary

The basis of all language, spoken and written, is words, and the aim of this chapter is to offer strategies for building vocabulary. Children are often 'lazy' in their choice of words. In a poem or a piece of descriptive writing they will tend to be satisfied with the first word that comes to mind. Thus 'big' is chosen as an adjective to describe an elephant, 'small' for a mouse, 'tiny' for an ant, and so on. These activities force children to consider a far wider range of possibilities.

At the heart of vocabulary building is the brainstorming activity. This is not an activity that comes naturally to children, and like any process needs to be taught. The most successful way to do this is by example, and strategies are suggested for class brainstorming. It is stressed that the teacher should be involved in this process and not simply act as a 'scribe'.

The vocabulary children know is often considerably larger than the vocabulary they use. A rule to offer children is 'Never be satisfied with your first choice of word. Brainstorm as many words as you can, then choose the best.' Best can variously be defined as the most appropriate, interesting or unusual, depending on the type of writing task.

A number of activities explore parts of speech. These activities, which focus on the use of adjectives, adverbs, prepositions and so on, are a far better means of understanding the function of the words than dry definitions or exercises.

SPEAKING AND
LISTENING

Images
a tropical forest
a rainy day

Adjectives
soaking
steaming

A CLASS BRAINSTORM

To build adventurousness in choosing words for a piece of creative writing.

†† *Whole class brainstorm, followed by class or groups.*

🕐 *30-minute class brainstorm, then open-ended writing.*

Key background information
Children will use a 'safe' vocabulary in their stories and poems, even though their knowledge of words can be quite wide. This exercise in brainstorming demonstrates the process of word building as an oral activity. It requires the teacher to be proactive in setting targets, encouraging participation and asking leading questions.

Resources needed
Chalkboard; writing materials.

What to do
In this activity your objective is to elicit from the children a range of words, phrases, ideas and images that they may find useful when writing a poem, and then write them up on the board so that the children can refer to them. The class must follow the 'hand-up' code when offering their suggestions.

In this activity, as in all brainstorming activities, the following guidelines apply. It is important that the teacher is

not merely a recorder of ideas from the children. He or she must engage in the process by:

▲ setting targets ('Can you think of ten adjectives to describe...?') *Note:* the first words and ideas will be the predictable ones, so always push for more;

▲ suggesting categories and listing headings ('What colours might you see when...?');

▲ asking for images ('What does that sound remind you of...?');

▲ being positive about inappropriate or humdrum ideas by asking the child to stretch the idea further;

▲ acting as a subtle filter/adapter/organiser.

It is always a good idea to ask the children to note their ideas down before they raise their hands. This ensures that they do not forget what they were going to say. It also allows them to think of new ideas while they are waiting to offer their suggestions.

Once the board is covered with words, ideas and images, work with the children on a class poem or ask them to work in groups to complete the writing. The writing process will involve:
Selecting the best of the words and images through discussion;
Shaping them into the final poem.

Suggestion(s) for extension
More capable children, or classes familiar with the brainstorming process, can develop the poem individually. In this case, do not exhaust the brainstorming process but leave some gaps for the children to continue to think of words and ideas before starting on the poem. This will reinforce the brainstorming process and give variety in the work produced.

Suggestion(s) for support
Ensure that less confident children are fully involved. Those who struggle to put ideas down on paper can often shine in a purely oral situation. If such children find it difficult to jot ideas down, ensure that you ask them for their ideas as quickly as possible, before a poor short-term memory allows the words to vanish from their minds.

If the class are unaccustomed to developing brainstorms into writing drafts, work on class poems first.

Assessment opportunities
This activity enables you to assess the range of children's vocabularies, and their adventurousness in using them in surprising and unusual ways.

Display ideas
The poems produced can be displayed, but it is also worthwhile to display the brainstorms and drafts created, thereby showing the writing process in action.

Other aspects of the English PoS covered
Writing – 1a, b, c; 2a, b, c, d, e; 3a, b, c.

ACTION POEMS

To build vocabulary in speech – participles.

†† *Whole class, followed by groups of three to five.*

🕐 *40 minutes.*

Key background information

Participles are action words and the extract from the poem on photocopiable page 150 provides many examples of them. It also serves as a model for the 'action poems' to be created by children in groups.

The emphasis in this activity is on poetry making and performing rather than poetry writing, although this will form part of the exercise.

Resources needed

Photocopiable page 150; writing materials; thesauruses.

What to do

Begin by reading the extract from 'The Cataract of Lodore' by Robert Southey on photocopiable page 150 with the class. A good approach is to read it aloud first, then provide copies for review. Alternatively, you may prefer to give out copies before you read it so that the chidren can follow it with you. Explain to the class that the 'ing' words in the poem are called participles. Participles can be simply defined as adjectives made from verbs.

Talk about the patterns in the poem. The poem starts with participles in pairs, then moves to groups of three, then finally groups of four, as the cataract becomes wider and wider.

Ask the children, in groups, to choose a suitable topic for their action poem. Some examples that can be offered are:

> A bicycle race; a bull in a china shop; an elephant in school; a storm at sea; an earthquake; a forest fire; an angry cook in a kitchen; a hopeless DIY enthusiast; a thunderstorm; an animal stampede; children at playtime; diggers on a building site; a football team.
>
> Quieter possibilities are: snow falling; butterflies in a garden.

Explain that you are not expecting anything on the scale of 'The Cataract of Lodore', but that they should make a list of all the possible participles that would suit their action poems, including actions by, say, onlookers. A section of a thunderstorm poem might be:

> People running and sheltering and complaining,
> Huddling and grumbling and umbrella-ing,
> Dogs barking and whining and hiding...

New words (neologisms) such as 'umbrella-ing' can be suggested if the children run out of ideas. They may also find it helpful to use thesauruses.

Once the children have made their lists they should work together in their groups to combine them into an action poem. These poems may be quite short, but encourage groups to use their words as imaginatively as possible.

Suggestion(s) for extension

Encourage children to think about the sound of the words. 'The Cataract of Lodore' has alliterative and onomatopoeic qualities. Suggest redrafts in which words with similar sounds are placed close together.

Suggestion(s) for support

Some children may need help with the word-building exercise. You or a support teacher should provide this by suggesting ideas. For instance, 'What noises can you hear from outside the playground? What about the birds that fly down once the children have left?'

Assessment opportunities

This activity is valuable for assessing both word building and performance skills.

Display/performance ideas

The action poems are excellent for performance, using individual or choral voices, or both, and varying the volume and expression depending on the actions taking place. Work with the groups on their performances.

Action poems

The cataract strong
Then plunges along,
Striking and raging
As if a way waging
Its caverns and rocks among.
Rising and leaping,
Sinking and creeping,
Swelling and sweeping,
Showering and springing,
Flying and flinging,
Writhing and ringing,
Eddying and whisking,
Spouting and frisking,
Turning and twisting,
Around and around
With endless rebound!
Smiting and fighting,
A sight to delight in;
Confounding, astounding,
Dividing and gliding and sliding,
And falling and brawling and sprawling,
And driving and riving and striving,
And sprinkling and twinkling and wrinkling,
And sounding and bounding and rounding,
And bubbling and troubling and doubling,
And grumbling and rumbling and tumbling,
And clattering and battering and shattering;
Retreating and beating and meeting and sheeting,
Delaying and straying and playing and spraying,
Advancing and prancing and glancing and dancing,
Recoiling, turmoiling and toiling and boiling,
And gleaming and streaming and steaming and beaming,
And rushing and flushing and brushing and gushing,
And flapping and rapping and clapping and slapping,
And curling and whirling and purling and twirling...

From The Cataract of Lodore by Robert Southey

The poems, with suitable illustrations, make excellent material for book making and display. Select some of the most original participles used and make a wall display with a heading 'Word list' for the class to use in their writing.

Other aspects of the English PoS covered
Writing – 1a, b, c; 2a, b, c, d, e; 3b, c.

Reference to photocopiable sheet
Photocopiable page 150 provides an extract from a poem which can be read to the class to initiate work on participles.

▣ THE ADJECTIVE GAME

To encourage imaginative uses and more appropriate choices of adjectives.
†† *Whole class.*
🕐 *45 minutes.*

Key background information
The English language is rich in descriptive words. A simple concept such as hot, wet, or angry is represented by a wide range of words, each with a different force or nuance. Under the word 'anger' a thesaurus lists: wrath, ire, fury, rage, dudgeon, huff, flare-up, passion, and many more. 'To be angry' has words such as seethe, simmer, sizzle, fume, fret, boil, storm, rave, rant, bluster and so on. All of these words have slightly different meanings or degrees of emphasis.

This activity should begin with a less abstract concept than anger. In the example below, 'hot' is suggested as a good starting word. The children are asked to brainstorm connected words, then put them in order.

Resources needed
Chalkboard. For the support activity – thesauruses.

What to do
Write the word 'hot' in the middle of the board. Ask the children for words that are similar to hot. Write these in a circle around the central idea. (See diagram below.)

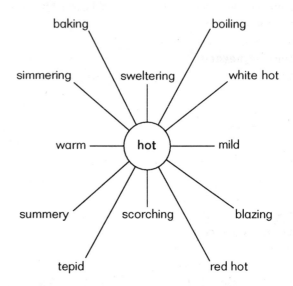

The older or more sophisticated the class, the more ideas you will have. Mild slang expressions can be included.

Now work with the class to list the words in order of 'hotness'. For some words, this is not particularly obvious (is 'red hot' hotter than 'scorching'?) and this can lead to much useful discussion.

Finally, work on a class poem about a hot day, or maybe a hot environment, such as a kitchen or an erupting volcano, using a selection of the words gathered in the brainstorm. A simple pattern is given below.

> It's warm,
> And the orange sun rises over the forest.
> It's hot,
> And the animals look for shelter.
> It's sweltering...

Suggestion(s) for extension
The object of this activity is to enable children to have the confidence to brainstorm a word list which they can then use when writing poems of their own. More confident children will be able to do this once the model has been provided. Other children may be happier working in groups or pairs. Good starter concepts for individuals are cold, wet, noisy, angry, fast, big. Children may also come up with their own starters.

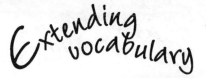
Suggestion(s) for support

The class work allows all children to contribute words or ideas of their own. A support teacher may help a group who require extra support, if they are working by themselves. A thesaurus will be a particularly useful aid to children needing support work.

Assessment opportunities

Look for children who are fully involved in the class discussion. More important even than this is the quality of the ideas they contribute.

Opportunities for IT

Let the children use a word processor to help them to order and structure the words that they have chosen into an order which depicts the varying degrees of hot or cold. Show them how to 'cut and paste' or 'drag and drop' the words to sequence them correctly. If the word processor has a thesaurus, the children can look up extra words and include them in their list. Bind together the final lists to make a class book of adjectives.

Display ideas

The final poems can be displayed on suitably coloured paper. The hot poem, for example, could start on light pink paper, and then progress to deeper shades of red paper as the poem gets 'hotter'.

THE ADVERB GAME

To increase understanding of the function of adverbs, and to extend vocabulary.

†† *Whole class.*

🕐 *An occasional five-minute 'one-off' activity.*

Previous skills/knowledge needed

The children will need to have a general background knowledge of parts of speech – nouns, verbs, adjectives – so that adverbs can be put into context. It is not necessary to 'teach' what an adverb is before the activity, as this is a good means of introducing it.

Key background information

The adverb has a range of functions. This activity focuses on the most straightforward, in which the adverb answers the question 'How was it done?' Most adverbs end in 'ly', but not all of them. Apart from teaching the meaning of adverbs in a light-hearted and amusing way, this activity develops confidence and quick thinking.

Creating *new* adverbs is an interesting part of this activity; most adjectives can be turned into adverbs by adding 'ly' to them. Nouns can sometimes also be made into adverbs with the addition of 'ily', for example 'he hissed snakily', 'she stared stonily'.

Resources needed

Chalkboard; writing materials.

What to do

Below is a list of simple activities. Write them on the board. Add to them if you wish.

▲ Walk across the room.

▲ Run on the spot.

▲ Crawl.

▲ Read a poem.

Now write up a list of adverbs. The box below has a useful selection, but you or the children can add to it.

fast slowly dreamily angrily sadly stupidly intelligently backwards peculiarly lazily snakily quietly noisily smoothly carefully carelessly hungrily amusingly importantly suspiciously tiredly annoyingly mechanically secretly tearfully nervously boldly happily jerkily frighteningly feebly badly well

Ask each child to select one of the activities written on the board and an adverb from the list. Then choose one of the children to do the activity 'in the manner of the adverb'. So a child may be asked to walk across the room lazily, sadly, intelligently, backwards, amusingly, importantly and so on. Clearly, some adverbs are easier to act than others, and some more appropriate to one activity than others.

Reading a poem backwards is more challenging than walking backwards! Each time an adverb is used, cross it out, so that it is used only once.

Finally, asking the children to write sentences including adverbs, and to draw pictures showing them in action, can reinforce their understanding and lead to display work (see 'Display ideas').

Suggestion(s) for extension
In a more challenging version of this activity the children choose the adverb themselves, then challenge the rest of the group to 'guess the adverb'.

Suggestion(s) for support
Some of the adverbs are quite difficult words. The children will benefit if they work with a teacher or support teacher on the meaning of adverbs, such as 'mechanically', before the activity starts.

Assessment opportunities
Look for correct and amusing interpretations of the meanings of the various adverbs, and the confidence shown in the performances when interpreting them.

Display ideas
Make an 'adverb display' showing a range of adverbs, and pictures or sentences produced by the class that demonstrate their meaning. It may be difficult to draw pictures of some adverbs which describe actions.

Other aspects of the English PoS covered
Reading – 3.
Writing – 2d; 3b.

FORMAL AND INFORMAL LANGUAGE

To increase understanding of formal and informal language.

✟✟ *Whole class, followed by pairs.*

🕑 *Two sessions of half-an-hour each.*

Key background information
Children often find it difficult to differentiate between situations requiring formal speech and those requiring informal. While over-formality has largely disappeared, certainly in the context of children's language, it is still important for children to develop an awareness of different language registers. This activity introduces the topic in an amusing way.

Resources needed
One copy per pair of photocopiable pages 151 and 152; writing materials; photocopiable assessment page 153 (as required).

What to do
Discuss with the class the general topic of formality and informality. If possible, relate an anecdote of your own when you 'got it wrong'. Unexpectedly finding yourself talking to someone important on the phone is a common example. The photocopiable sheets feature six situations, three formal and three informal. Three of them (on the first sheet) have the speech bubbles filled in with inappropriate language. Give each pair of children a copy of photocopiable page 151. Ask them, working in their pairs, to think of speech which is more appropriate for each situation. After they have discussed the three pictures thoroughly, tell the children to write down the words which they think would provide appropriate speech (writing in the box on the right-hand side of each scene).

Then give the children copies of photocopiable page 152 (again, working in pairs). Ask them to fill in the blank speech bubbles after discussing each situation with their partners.

When the children have finished their writing, explain that you would like them to work on an improvisation on one of the six situations taken from the photocopiable sheets. They can develop their improvisation using either appropriate or inappropriate speech. Emphasise that they must make it clear whether they are using formal speech or informal speech and stress the importance of conveying whether the speech is appropriate for their chosen situation.

This activity can lead to story writing involving direct speech.

Suggestion(s) for extension
The situations on the photocopiable sheets are, to some extent, stereotypical and exaggerated – it is not every day that one meets the Prime Minister! Extend the activity with

enabling children to think about appropriate language when dealing with others. Assessing the development of this important social skill will need to be done over a period of time. This activity is also appropriate for summative assessment and a photocopiable sheet is provided for this purpose.

Display ideas
Make a formal/informal display, including writing, 'cartoon' style drawings and a poster showing 'class manners'.

Other aspects of the English PoS covered
Writing – 1a, b, c; 2a, b, c; 3a.

Reference to photocopiable sheets
Photocopiable pages 151 and 152 offer six situations, three on each sheet, in which either formal or informal speech is appropriate. On the first sheet the language shown in the speech bubbles is inappropriate for each situation; there is space for the children to write their own words – words which are suitable – alongside the pictures. The second sheet gives children a selection of different circumstances, each one requiring either formal or informal speech. The children respond by writing in the speech bubbles. The children then choose one situation (from either of the photocopiable sheets) on which to base an improvisation.

Photocopiable page 153 provides a record sheet for summative assessment.

WHO'S ON THE PHONE?

To gain further practice in formal and informal language.

†† *Improvisation in pairs, with class as audience.*

🕐 *A short 'filler' or a more extended activity.*

Key background information
This activity focuses on developing formal and informal language and is a good follow-up to the previous activity. If that activity has not been undertaken first, begin this activity with a class discussion on formal and informal language. This is a 'fun' activity in which one child receives an unexpected phone call from one of the characters. It can be linked with 'Police, quickly!' (page 40) and 'Junk phone call' (page 73), which are other telephone activities.

Preparation
Make up a set of cards, each with the name of a 'caller' on it. Suggested callers are:
▲ a friend,
▲ a grandparent;
▲ someone trying to sell something;
▲ a policeman;
▲ someone from the bank;

discussion on more realistic situations which are not quite so clear cut – situations involving relatives and visitors; and situations which require politeness in dealing with adults and other children. Helping a new class member is a situation that might be considered.

Suggestion(s) for support
The formal/informal concept is a difficult one for many children. Some general work on politeness and manners, perhaps leading to a simple set of class guidelines for a poster, might be helpful.

Assessment opportunities
Some children will have an instinctive 'feel' for appropriate language registers for different situations, while others will not yet have developed this. The activity can act as a trigger,

▲ a shopkeeper;

▲ the headteacher;

▲ a 'boss';

▲ a famous celebrity;

▲ the President of the United States.

Bear in mind that it is important to achieve a range of formal and informal telephone calls so choose suitable callers accordingly. Further cards can be made to represent people known to the children. A blank 'wild card' is a possiblity.

Resources needed

A set of 'caller' cards, one card for each pair (see 'Preparation'); two telephones, or suitable props to act as phones (alternatively, these can be mimed). Cassette recorder and writing materials (optional).

What to do

Hand out one of the pictures to the child who is the 'caller'. Tell the caller to ring up and talk to his or her partner in the manner of the character on the card; the child's partner will not know who is ringing until the telephone is 'answered'. Explain that they should then improvise a 'formal' or 'informal' conversation. The calls can be given a limited time of a couple of minutes, or you could bring the conversations to a close once the children start to flounder. Follow up the calls with a brief class discussion on how well both children managed to adopt the right degree of formality or informality.

The activity can develop into scripting work. Use a cassette recorder to record the improvised conversations, then ask the children involved to transcribe and rework their conversation to make a script.

Suggestion(s) for extension

Give the children a more complicated situation, involving the use of three telephones. One of the children has a 'formal' character on one line, and an 'informal' one on the other. The object is to try to talk to both of them, using the appropriate register. The three-way phone call can develop into an amusing situation when the wrong register is used by mistake, scandalising the 'formal' character!

Suggestion(s) for support

This is a task requiring considerable self-assurance. Less confident children should be allowed some planning time first, or should practise with a teacher or support teacher acting as their 'caller'.

Assessment opportunities

Look out for the individual child's deftness in handling appropriate register.

Performance ideas

If the conversations are scripted, polished performances can be given to another class or group.

Other aspects of the English PoS covered

Writing – 3a.

THE PREPOSITION GAME

To build confidence in using prepositions.

†† *Whole class or groups (with individuals taking turns).*

🕐 *A five-minute activity or a more extended one involving written work.*

Key background information

Prepositions are important words, but not easy to define. 'Positioning words' is a good, simple definition.

Preparation

Make copies of photocopiable pages 154 and 155 on to thin card. Cut out the individual words and put nouns in one bag, and prepositions in another.

Resources needed

Set of preposition and noun cards (made from photocopiable pages 154 and 155); two bags (or suitable holders).

What to do

Explain to the children that they are going to play 'The preposition game'. Show them the bags containing the preposition cards and noun cards, and ask each child in turn to draw out two noun cards and one preposition card. When they have picked out the three word cards, explain that their task is to make up an instant sentence combining the two

nouns and the preposition, inserting as many other words as they wish. For example:

> The tiny bus drove under the elephant.
> The burglar hid from the dog behind a tree.

Some combinations will be easier than others! The children may include more nouns in their sentences to give greater variety. Replace the nouns in the bag each time, but retain the prepositions until all of them have been used. This ensures that they are all incorporated.

Suggestion(s) for extension
Older and more able children can write 'Preposition poems'. Here is a wind poem using a wide range of prepositions:

> Wind, wind, where do you blow?
> Over the hills and under the stars,
> Through the forests and round the mountains,
> Behind the dustbins and inside the old tramp's coat...
> And in your dreams.

Poems could describe journeys, races, the sea. Other, more abstract ideas are also possible.

Suggestion(s) for support
To introduce the idea of the preposition to younger children or children requiring support, the following class activity is useful. Prepare a set of classroom shelves by placing a number of objects on them. Use the list of prepositions to ensure that some objects are under others, some behind, some on, some with, some in, and so on. ('Through' can be achieved by using a small hoop; 'off' by having a lid off its box.)

Give out a set of the preposition words or write them up. Ask the children, perhaps working in pairs, to use the words to explain where each object is. Once the children are familiar with the use of the prepositions, they can move on to the main activity.

Assessment opportunities
Look for clear understanding of the meaning and function of the various prepositions introduced.

Display ideas
A valuable language display idea is to write out larger versions of the words on to card and display them on the 'preposition' shelves, next to the matching objects.

Other aspects of the English PoS covered
Reading – 3.
Writing – 2d; 3b, c.

Reference to photocopiable sheets
Photocopiable pages 154 and 155 provide a set of words – nouns and prepositions – which are used to make cards to play 'The preposition game'.

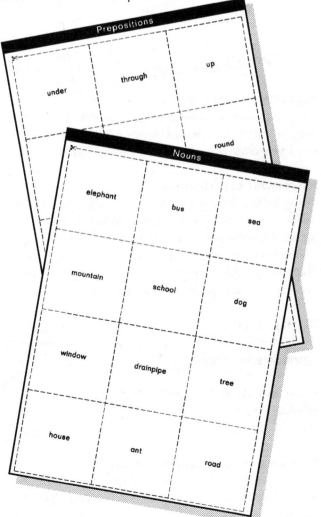

Prepositions

under   through   up
round

Nouns

elephant   bus   sea
mountain   school   dog
window   drainpipe   tree
house   ant   road

SPEAKING AND
LISTENING

SPECIAL WORDS

To build confidence in handling a specialist vocabulary.

†† *Pairs.*

🕐 *30 minutes.*

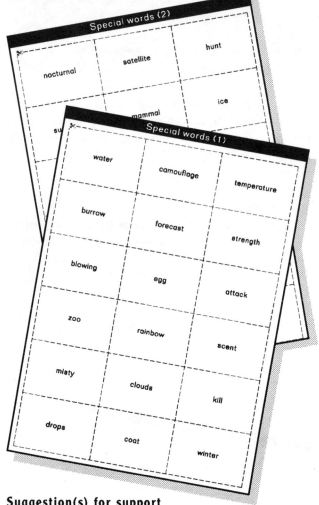

Key background information

All curriculum subjects have their own 'special' vocabulary. This is particularly true, of course, of science. Children need to broaden their knowledge of such vocabulary, and feel confident in applying it. This activity uses a mix of words taken from reference books about weather and animals. Of course, many words will be appropriate to either subject, although some uses are sophisticated or metaphorical.

Resources needed

One copy per pair of photocopiable pages 156 and 157; scissors; dictionaries.

What to do

Give out the scissors and copies of photocopiable pages 156 and 157 to each pair. Tell the children to cut out the words and then make three piles: 'weather', 'animals' and 'both'. Some words will be easy to allocate, while others are more difficult. All will require discussion, and the use of a dictionary if necessary. Once the words have been allocated, discuss with the whole class the choices they have made, exploring particularly any differences of opinion.

Suggestion(s) for extension

A more sophisticated activity involves groups of three. Nominate one child for weather, and another for animals. The third child is a 'judge'. Tell the judge to turn up the words one at a time and ask the other two to argue the case for including the word in their pile. In some cases, the arguments may have to be very far-fetched! The judge then decides which child has made the best case. That child will 'win' the word. The winner is the child with most words.

Suggestion(s) for support

A support group can carry out the paired activity with a support teacher, the teacher prompting with questions – 'Does this word have anything to do with the weather? What about...?'

Assessment opportunities

The more sophisticated the pairs, the larger the 'both' pile will be as they will think of a broader range of possible uses for words. In the extension activity, assess how successful the children are at putting forward their case, and how sophisticated their arguments are. Listen out for abstract and metaphorical usage of the various words.

Display ideas

'Special' vocabulary lists make a very practical display, with appropriate illustrations.

Other aspects of the English PoS covered

Reading – 1b, 2c.
Writing – 3b, c.

Reference to photocopiable sheets

Photocopiable pages 156 and 157 provide a set of words which can be divided between the headings 'weather', 'animals' and 'both'.

Photocopiables

The pages in this section can be photocopied for use in the classroom or school which has purchased this book, and do not need to be declared in any return in respect of any photocopying licence.

They comprise a varied selection of both pupil and teacher resources, including pupil worksheets, resource material and record sheets to be completed by the teacher or children. Most of the photocopiable pages are related to individual activities in the book; the name of the activity is indicated at the top of the sheet, together with a page reference indicating where the lesson plan for that activity can be found.

Individual pages are discussed in detail within each lesson plan, accompanied by ideas for adaptation where appropriate – of course, each sheet can be adapted to suit your own needs and those of your class. Sheets can also be coloured, laminated, mounted on to card, enlarged and so on where appropriate.

Photocopiable record sheets (indicated by the ◈ icon) which accompany the summative assessment activities throughout the book have spaces provided for children's names and for noting the date on which each sheet was used. This means that, if so required, they can be included easily within any pupil assessment portfolio.

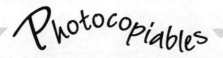

Giving a talk, see page 17

My talk

My talk is about:

▲ Overview: _____

_____

▲ My main points are:

1 _____

2 _____

3 _____

4 _____

▲ What I want to say about 1: _____

_____

▲ What I want to say about 2: _____

_____

▲ What I want to say about 3: _____

_____

▲ What I want to say about 4: _____

_____

▲ My final sentence will be: _____

_____

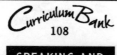

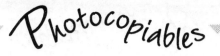

Giving a talk, see page 17

Information handling

Name: _____ Age: _____

Class: _____ Date of assessment: _____

Comments on skill in information handling skills:	
Can speak confidently to an audience.	
Can speak with clear diction and appropriate intonation.	
Can use standard English effectively.	
Can speak with awareness of standard grammatical constructions.	
Can provide an overview of the subject matter.	
Can organise factual material in an effective way.	
Can provide an effective conclusion to a talk.	
Can use a 'specialist' vocabulary effectively.	
General comments:	

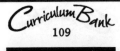
SPEAKING AND LISTENING

Photocopiables

Information bank

elephants

oak trees

athletics

cars

instruments

looking after a pet

the moon

computers

France

healthy food

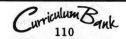

Zoo notices, see page 20

Metropolis Wildlife Park

Wombat

SPEAKING AND
LISTENING

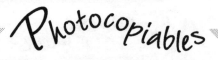

Looking at pictures, see page 21

Looking at pictures

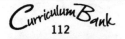

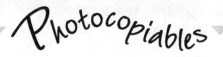

A special day, see page 27

A special day

▲ Where did you go? _____

▲ How did you get there? _____

▲ Who did you go with? _____

▲ What did you see? _____

_____

_____

▲ What did you do? _____

_____

_____

▲ Did anything funny happen? _____

_____

_____

▲ Is there anything else you
would like to tell the class about?

_____

_____

_____

_____

SPEAKING AND
LISTENING

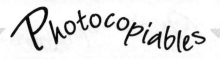

Explaining a technology project, see page 33

Explaining and understanding

Name: _____ Age: _____

Class: _____ Date of assessment: _____

Comments on ability in explaining and understanding skills:	
Can speak confidently to an audience.	
Can speak with clear diction and appropriate intonation.	
Can use standard English effectively.	
Can speak with awareness of standard grammatical constructions.	
Can work effectively with a partner.	
Can clearly state objectives at the outset.	
Can explain a process clearly and logically.	
Can make a clear assessment of the outcome.	
Can respond effectively to questions.	
General comments:	

SPEAKING AND LISTENING

How it works, see page 35

How it works

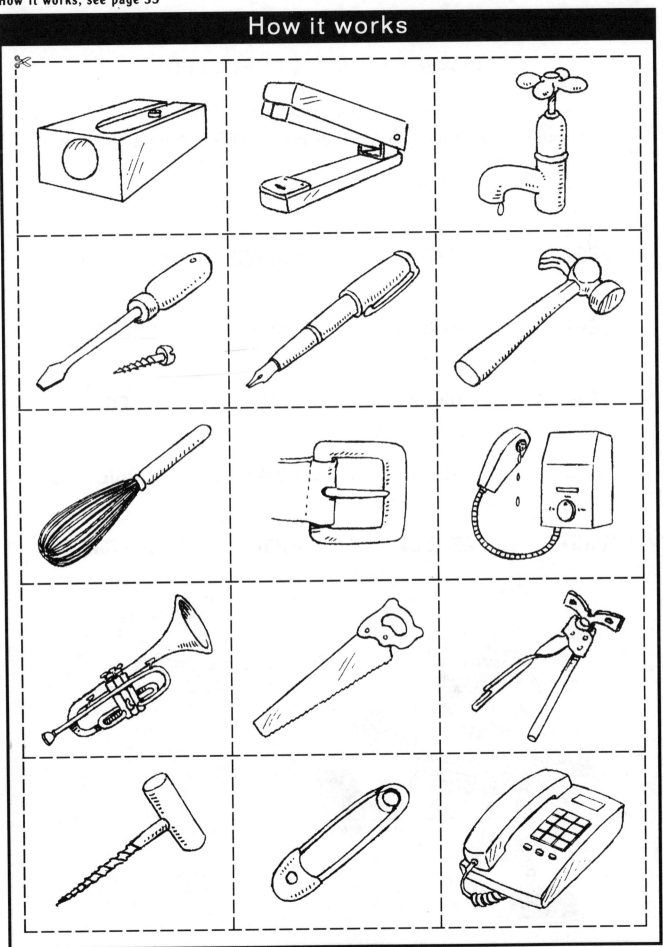

SPEAKING AND
LISTENING

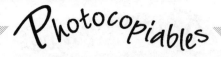

The robot game, see page 37

The robot game

CLANK and RATTLE ROBOT Ltd

Instructions

Congratulations on buying a CLANK and RATTLE robot! The robot will respond to these words only. Using combinations of these words, your new robot can carry out many different tasks!

FAST	LIFT	FORWARDS	BACKWARDS
LEFT	RIGHT	RAISE	LOWER
STOP	WALK	ARM	LEG
HAND	TURN	STRETCH	SLOWLY
TWIST	OBJECT	GRASP	RELEASE

SPEAKING AND
LISTENING

Describing a picture, see page 38

Describing a picture (1)

SPEAKING AND
LISTENING

Describing a picture, see page 38

Describing a picture (2)

How to describe a picture.
1. Say what the whole picture is about.
2. Describe the most important things in the picture, and say where they are, using the grid, indicating top left, bottom centre, etc.
3. Describe important details in the picture, saying where they are.

Using a map

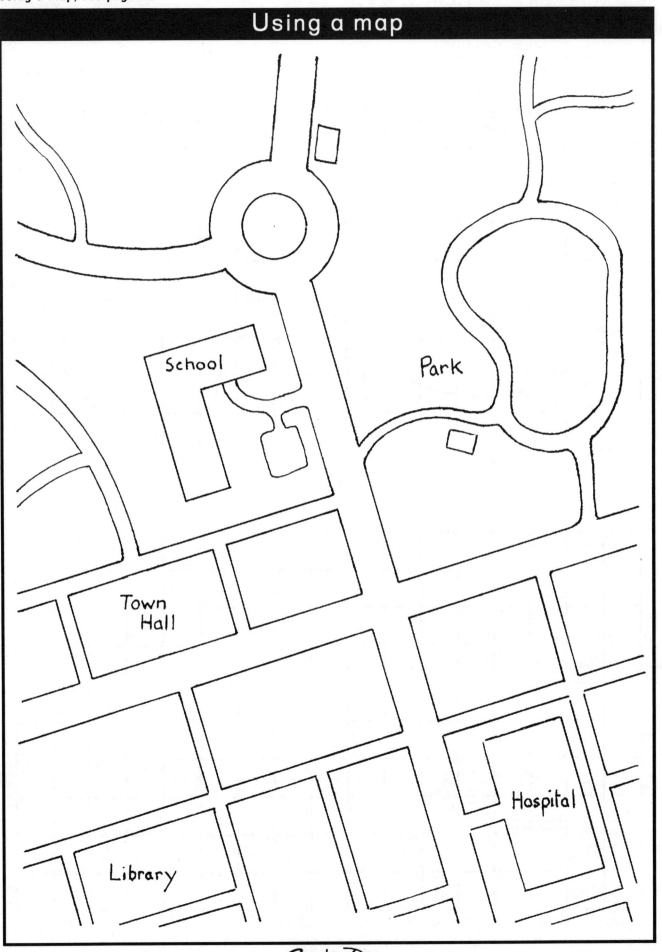

School

Park

Town
Hall

Hospital

Library

Talking about maths

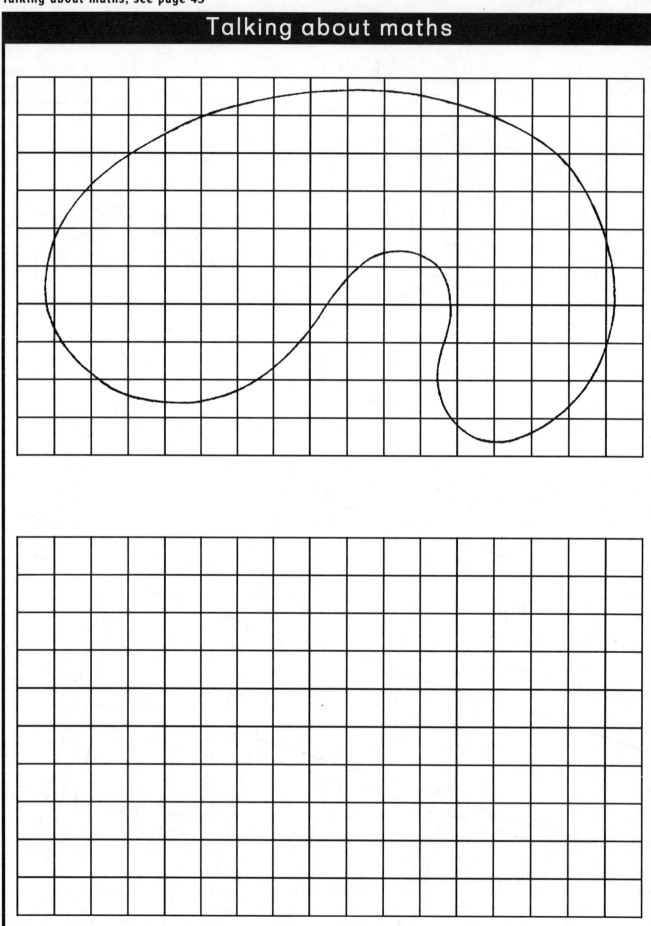

SPEAKING AND LISTENING

Agony aunt, see page 46

Any problems?

INTRODUCER Welcome to *Any problems!* Here is your problem solver, Caneye Helpyoo!

CANEYE Hello everyone. Well, the phones are already ringing. My first problem comes from Mike Smith, of London. Hello Mike, what is your problem?

MIKE Hello Caneye. This is my problem. My parents keep on and on about my untidy bedroom. The thing is, I like it as it is! What can I do?

CANEYE Take your parents down to their garden shed or into their garage if they have one. They are usually a mess! Tell them that you'll tidy your bedroom when they tidy up their mess!

MIKE But the shed and garage are spotless!

CANEYE Oh dear. It looks as if you're stuck. Happy tidying, Mike! Now here's Tracy from Birmingham.

TRACY Hello, Caneye. I've got a big problem. My dog bit the postman's fingers when he pushed the letters through the door. Now he won't deliver letters any more.

CANEYE You need a small cage on the inside of your letter box to catch the letters in, and a big box of chocs for your postman! Next problem please!

GARETH Hello, I'm Gareth from Wales. I've got horrible neighbours who throw slugs and snails over my fence. They are eating my vegetables! What can I do?

CANEYE Collect up all the slugs and snails. Cook them up in a stew with the munched vegetables. Invite your neighbours round for dinner and serve up your slug and snail stew. That ought to stop them! Now, who's next?

EPPIE My name is Eppie, from Scotland. My little sister is always borrowing my T-shirts without asking. I'm getting really annoyed!

CANEYE Well, you could put a burglar alarm on your wardrobe, or itching powder in your T-shirts. If you wore all your T-shirts all the time, she wouldn't be able to get hold of them! Now we've got William on the line.

WILLIAM My problem is this. My grandmother still treats me as if I'm seven years old. Last Christmas she gave me a teddy bear!

CANEYE How old are you, William?

WILLIAM Twenty-six!

SPEAKING AND LISTENING

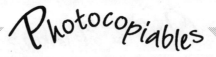

Behind the door

▲ What will happen when the door is opened?

SPEAKING AND
LISTENING

Building up pictures, see page 48

Building up pictures

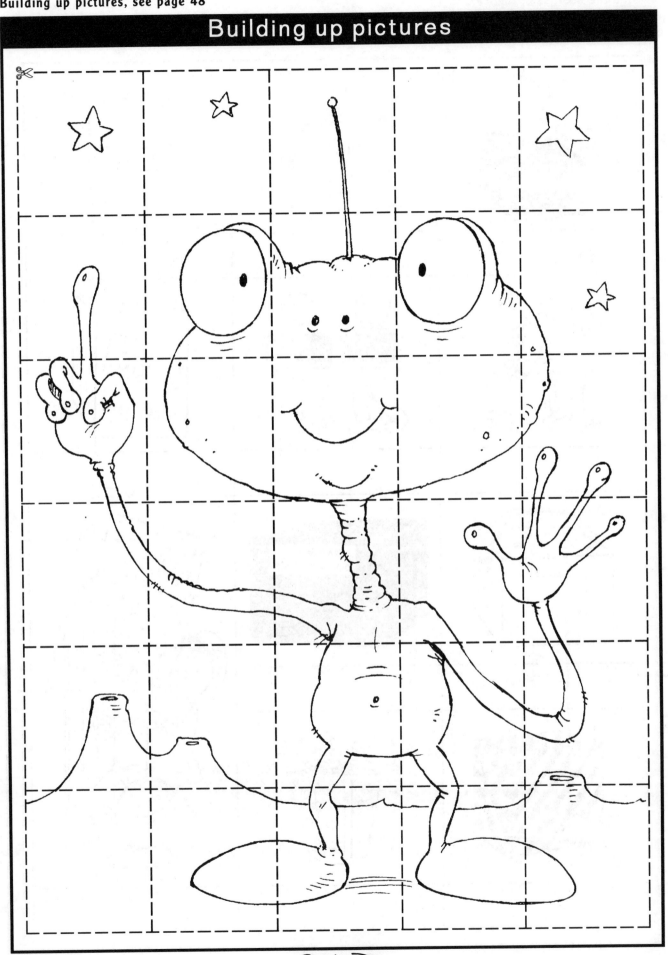

SPEAKING AND LISTENING

What's in the parcel?, see page 50

What's in the parcel?

THIS WAY UP

FRAGILE

KEEP COOL

DANGER DO NOT OPEN

TO: THE QUEEN

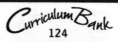
SPEAKING AND LISTENING

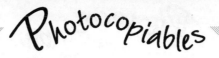

What's in the parcel?, see page 50

Reasoning and speculating

Name: _____ Age: _____

Class: _____ Date of assessment: _____

Comments on skill in reasoning and speculating:	
Can work effectively with a partner.	
Can made deductions from evidence.	
Can speculate in an imaginative way.	
Can use standard English effectively.	
Can speak with awareness of standard grammatical constructions.	
Can use persuasive language effectively.	
Can offer and justify opinions.	
Can organise a presentation in an effective way.	
General comments:	

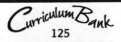
SPEAKING AND LISTENING

Being a detective, see page 51

The case of the left-handed teacher (1)

Sherlock Jones was examining the battered briefcase with his magnifying glass. Dr Wotnot had already inspected it but could find no clues about its owner.

'I can't see anything remarkable about it at all, Jones,' he said. 'It's just a battered old empty briefcase. It could have belonged to anyone.'

'You see the same things as I do, Wotnot, but you do not make deductions,' smiled Jones. 'Though I agree, there is not much evidence here. Apart, of course, from the obvious facts that the case belonged to a left-handed, hard-working schoolteacher, who is much less careful than she used to be with her belongings. She travels to work by bicycle and is fond of jam sandwiches.'

'What!' cried Dr Wotnot in astonishment. 'How can you possibly know those things?'

'Elementary, my dear Wotnot!' replied Jones.

▲ How might Sherlock Jones have found out so much about the owner of the briefcase? Discuss.

SPEAKING AND LISTENING

Being a detective, see page 51

The case of the left-handed teacher (2)

'The marks left by the fingers on the handle show that it was most often carried in the left hand. As it was very heavy, this is almost certainly the owner's strongest hand. We know the owner was a schoolteacher because of the layer of chalk dust on the case, and she worked hard because the case is so out of shape – every night the teacher struggled home with a great pile of books to mark. We know this person has become careless because the case has been patched, but more recently the patches have come loose and have not been repaired. The case shows clear signs of strap marks, the sort of straps used to attach cases to bicycles.'

'But what about the jam sandwiches?' cried Wotnot. 'Surely you are joking about that!'

Sherlock Jones pointed to a sticky patch inside the case.

'Strawberry jam,' he said. 'Had there been any traces of sugar, I would have said doughnuts. No sugar clearly indicates sandwiches. As I said, my dear Wotnot, it's elementary!'

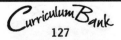
SPEAKING AND LISTENING

How did it happen?, see page 53

How did it happen?

SPEAKING AND
LISTENING

What are they saying?, see page 54

What are they saying?

SPEAKING AND LISTENING

Who owns what?, see page 55

Who owns what?

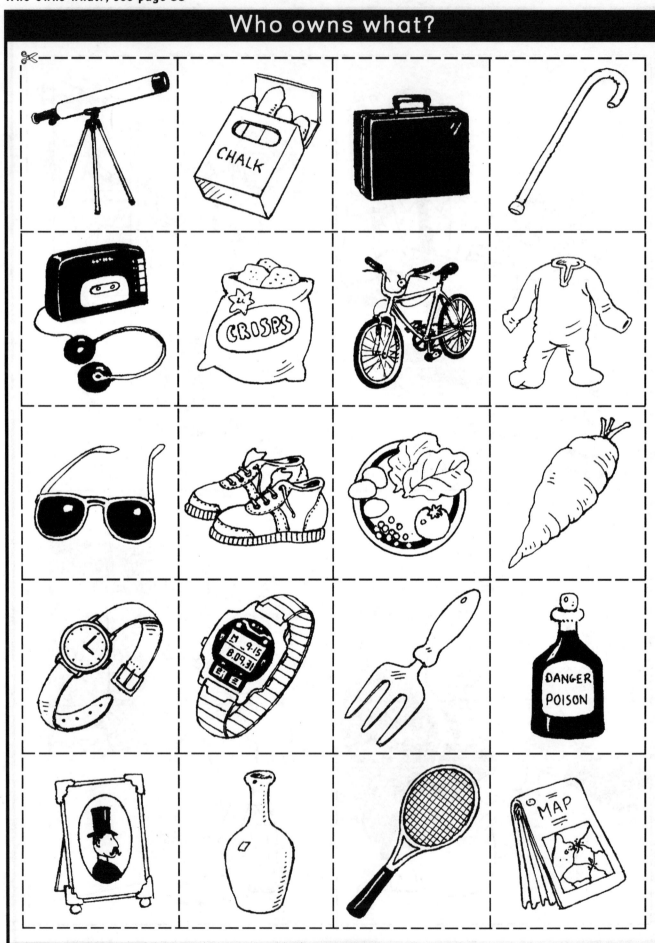

Photocopiables

Keep safe!

Cleaning the car, see page 65

Clean that car!

MUM/DAD	The car is absolutely filthy! I haven't got time to clean it and the car wash is closed. Could you clean it for me?
JIM/GEMMA	But it's my favourite TV programme! It doesn't matter if the car is dirty. We don't eat our dinner off the car!
MUM/DAD	Of course it matters! Look, I'll give you 30p if you'll give the car a really good clean. You can wait until after your programme. I'll find you a bucket of hot water and a sponge.
JIM/GEMMA	30p! That's not very much! It costs £2 in the car wash so I want £2 as well. Otherwise I'm not budging!
MUM/DAD	But you won't clean it as well as the car wash. You always forget to do the wheels. Besides, what do you need £2 for?
JIM/GEMMA	Lots of things. I promise I'll do a really good job for £2.
MUM/DAD	What about 50p?
JIM/GEMMA	No!
MUM/DAD	All right, I'll make it a pound. That's my final offer!
JIM/GEMMA	I'll do it for £1.50. And that's *my* final offer!

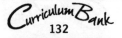
SPEAKING AND LISTENING

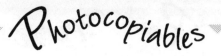
Cleaning the car, see page 65

I want... and please can I...?

Please can I stay up late?	Tidy your bedroom!
I want a pet crocodile!	The grass needs cutting!
I need more pocket money!	Come and help with the washing-up!
I want to go swimming!	Stop teasing your brother!
I don't want to go to school!	You can't wear that T-shirt!
I want chips for tea!	Those trainers are too expensive!

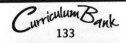

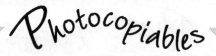

Questionnaire: your town

▲ Which of these best describes the town or city you live in, or the one nearest to you?

☐	An exciting place to live
☐	An ordinary place to live
☐	Not a very interesting place to live

☐	Good sports facilities
☐	Average sports facilities
☐	Not very good sports facilities

☐	Many good shops
☐	Some good shops
☐	Not many good shops

☐	Plenty of entertainment
☐	Some entertainment
☐	Not much entertainment

☐	A good bus service
☐	Reasonable bus service
☐	Poor bus service

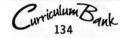

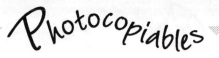

The ark game, see page 69

Opinion and persuasion

Name: _____ Age: _____

Class: _____ Date of assessment: _____

Comments on skill in persuasion and giving opinions:	
Can use persuasive language effectively.	
Can give information in a logical and ordered way.	
Can offer and justify opinions.	
Can speak with fluency, confidence and awareness of audience.	
Can use standard English effectively.	
Can speak with awareness of standard grammatical constructions.	
Can speak with clear diction and appropriate intonation.	
Can organise a presentation in an effective way.	
General comments:	

SPEAKING AND LISTENING

I think that..., see page 75

I think that...

Cutting down forests

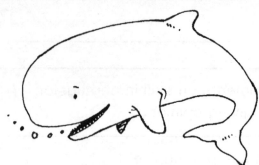

Killing whales

Polluting factories

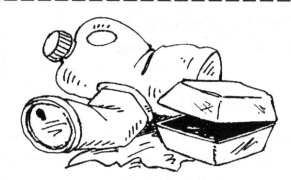

Litter

Eating junk food

New roads

Animal cruelty

Wild card

SPEAKING AND LISTENING

Save our pond!, see page 76

Croakers pond factsheet

Croakers pond is situated on the last piece of open land in the city. Despite some pollution from the nearby car factory, it still has a wide range of wildlife. Water beetles and water boatmen are seen in the water. Many frogs and newts live in the pond. The frogs return each year from surrounding gardens to breed. Many butterflies, dragonflies and birds live around the pond. Migrating water birds use the pond to break their long journeys. Over 100 species of plants grow here, including a rare orchid.

The land is owned by the Smog motor company. They have allowed schools and local wildlife clubs to visit the pond over the years and use it as an unofficial nature reserve. Many schools depend on it for their science work. Now the company needs the land for a new building to make a new range of high performance cars. 'We are very sorry,' the company said, 'But it is our land and we can do what we like with it. The pond will be filled in at the end of the month.'

Getting the message across

▲ Raise money for your campaign.
▲ Write to your local newspaper.
▲ Contact TV and radio stations.
▲ Write to local groups and seek their support.
▲ Design and print leaflets and posters.
▲ Write to important people – your MP, the government, the council.
▲ Write to important and well-known people who are concerned about the environment.
▲ Organise protests and 'stunts' that will attract the media.

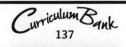

SPEAKING AND LISTENING

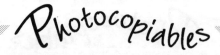

Tricky customers, see page 78

The super salesman

SALESMAN Good morning, madam. I am working in the area introducing a wonderful range of new brushes that will help you do your housework in half the time...

LADY AT THE DOOR I don't need any brushes, thank you.

SALESMAN I'm sure you have plenty of ordinary brushes. But I'm sure you haven't got anything like the brushes I have here in my case! These are brand new from America and can change your life...

LADY AT THE DOOR Look, I've told you. I don't want to buy any brushes.

SALESMAN Buy? Who said anything about buy? I'm not here to sell you anything. I am just demonstrating these wonderful new inventions, as a special service to you! All I want from you, madam, is five minutes of your valuable time...

LADY AT THE DOOR I'm busy.

SALESMAN ...and in exchange for that you will receive a valuable free gift, yours to keep with no obligation! What have you got to lose?

LADY AT THE DOOR What valuable free gift?

SALESMAN Well, now, they are at the bottom of my case. Just let me come in and give you a quick demonstration...

[*Ten minutes later.*]

SALESMAN Well, that will be twenty-six pounds altogether!

LADY AT THE DOOR What about my free gift?

SALESMAN Oh yes! Here you are. A free full-colour sixty-page catalogue of further bargains from our wonderful range. All available on special credit terms!

SPEAKING AND LISTENING

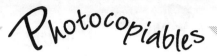

No thank you, see page 79

Joining the gang

JOE It's easy! Just look around the shop to find something she's run out of. Ask her for that so she has to go into the back of the shop. Then take the sweets and put them in your pocket. Just take one of each so that she doesn't notice they're missing.

CHRIS What if I get caught?

SAMANTHA You won't get caught!

JOE You've got to do it. Otherwise you can't be in the gang. It's a test. We've all done it.

SAMANTHA If you don't do it, it proves you're a chicken. We don't have chickens in our gang!

JOE [*acts like a chicken*] Cluck, cluck, cluck!

SAMANTHA Go on, do it now. If you don't we'll tell the whole class you're just a baby!

JOE A baby chicken! Cluck cluck!

SPEAKING AND LISTENING

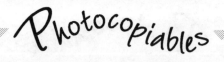

Story quiz

▲ Can you remember the following?

▲ What was the story called?

_____

▲ Who wrote it?

_____

▲ What are the names of the main characters?

_____

_____

▲ Where did the story take place?

_____

▲ Which bit of the story did you enjoy the most?

I enjoyed it when...

_____

_____

_____

SPEAKING AND
LISTENING

Whose shoes?, see page 85

Whose shoes?

SPEAKING AND
LISTENING

Story starts, see page 88

Places

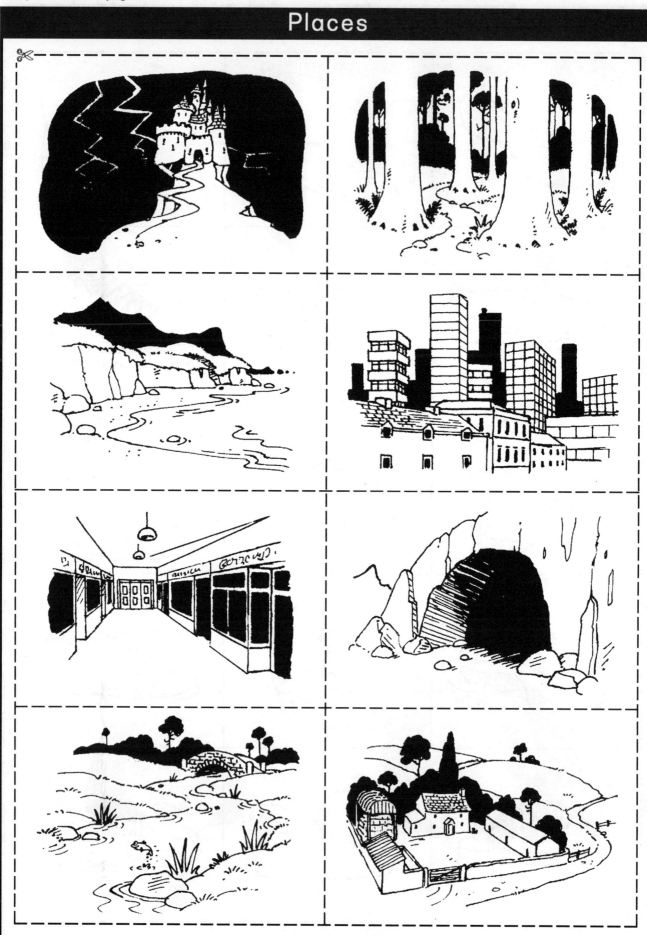

SPEAKING AND LISTENING

Story starts, see page 88

People

SPEAKING AND LISTENING

Story starts, see page 88

Objects

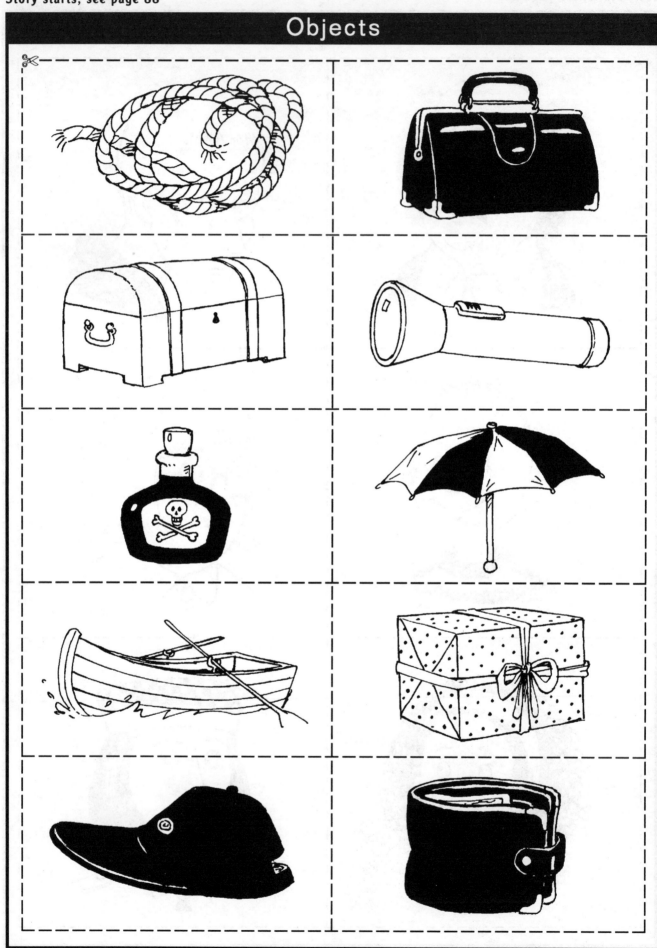

SPEAKING AND LISTENING

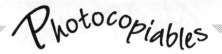
Make a play, see page 89

The secret of Spiderweb Castle

Setting: Spiderweb Castle

Time: Midnight

[*The gang are creeping through a window of Spiderweb Castle, an old ruin with a bad reputation.*]

LIAM   I wish I was still at home.

TONI   Don't be such a baby!

GEETA   I bet there are hundreds of ghosts in this old place.

SAM   I can see someone! He's just standing there, not moving...

TONI   Shine your torch, Sam.

SAM   It's just a suit of armour!

LIAM   Let's go home!

GEETA   Oh, shut up, Liam. Let's try the next room.

[*They pass through a doorway into another gloomy room. There is a creaking noise and a crash as the door slams shut behind them.*]

TONI   We're locked in. There isn't another way out!

LIAM   I knew this was a bad idea.

SAM   Where's Geeta?

TONI   She was here a minute ago. She seems to have disappeared into thin air!

[*They hear footsteps in the distance, coming closer and closer...*]

Make a play, see page 89

Trapped!

Setting: A seaside cave.   Time: Just before high tide.

[*The gang are on a seaside holiday.*]

TONI   Let's explore this cave. It seems to go back a really long way.

LIAM   It's a bit dark!

SAM   Of course it's dark. It's a cave. Anyway, I've got my torch.

GEETA   Phew! What a smell of rotten seaweed!

LIAM   Let's go back. It must be dinner time and I'm hungry.

TONI   What's that shiny thing on the ground?

SAM   It's a gold ring! I wonder how that got here?

GEETA   Maybe it's a treasure cave.

TONI   It must have been dropped by someone exploring the cave.

[*A strange gushing noise is heard.*]

LIAM   What's that noise?

[*Sam turns and flashes a torch behind them.*]

SAM   Water!

GEETA   It's the sea coming in! We forgot about the tide!

LIAM   We're trapped! Help! Help!

TONI   Shut up, Liam. We're in trouble, gang. Any ideas?

SPEAKING AND
LISTENING

Round robin

The forest animals were nervous. They could smell smoke...

The children knew that they were in real trouble now...

When Lauren got on the bus, she found her money had gone...

The class had no idea what an extraordinary day it was going to be...

Picture story, see page 92

Picture story

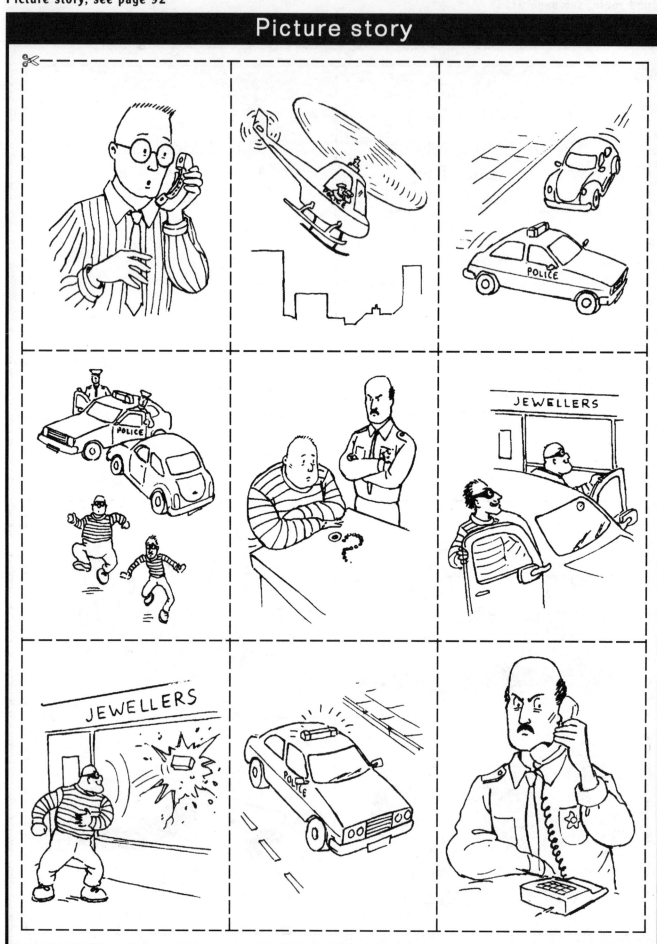

SPEAKING AND LISTENING

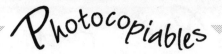

Storytelling and performance

Name: _____ Age: _____

Class: _____ Date of assessment: _____

Comments on listening skills:	
Can listen attentively to a short story told by the teacher.	
Can listen and respond to a story on tape/CD.	
Can concentrate on listening despite distractions.	
Can listen and respond to instructions effectively.	
Can understand and retell the sequence of events in a simple narrative.	
Can understand and comment on the motives of characters in a story.	
Can predict outcomes in a narrative.	
Can make deductions from evidence heard in a story.	
General comments:	

SPEAKING AND LISTENING

Action poems

The cataract strong
Then plunges along,
Striking and raging
As if a way waging
Its caverns and rocks among:
Rising and leaping,
Sinking and creeping,
Swelling and sweeping,
Showering and springing,
Flying and flinging,
Writhing and ringing,
Eddying and whisking,
Spouting and frisking,
Turning and twisting,
Around and around
With endless rebound!
Smiting and fighting,
A sight to delight in;
Confounding, astounding,
Dividing and gliding and sliding,
And falling and brawling and sprawling,
And driving and riving and striving,
And sprinkling and twinkling and wrinkling,
And sounding and bounding and rounding,
And bubbling and troubling and doubling,
And grumbling and rumbling and tumbling,
And clattering and battering and shattering;
Retreating and beating and meeting and sheeting,
Delaying and straying and playing and spraying,
Advancing and prancing and glancing and dancing,
Recoiling, turmoiling and toiling and boiling,
And gleaming and streaming and steaming and beaming,
And rushing and flushing and brushing and gushing,
And flapping and rapping and clapping and slapping,
And curling and whirling and purling and twirling...

From *The Cataract of Lodore* by Robert Southey

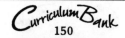

Formal and informal language (1)

Formal and informal language (2)

SPEAKING AND
LISTENING

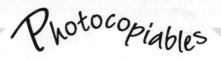

Formal and informal language, see page 102

Extending vocabulary

Name: _____ Age: _____

Class: _____ Date of assessment: _____

Comments on the child's skill in situations requiring different speech registers:	
Can use standard English effectively.	
Can speak with awareness of standard grammatical constructions.	
Can speak with clear diction and appropriate intonation.	
Can speak to adults with confidence.	
Can differentiate between formal and informal situations.	
Can use appropriate language and register when speaking to a range of people.	
General comments:	

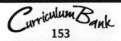

The preposition game, see page 104

Prepositions

under	through	up
down	behind	round
over	on	by
with	off	near

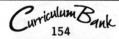

SPEAKING AND
LISTENING

The preposition game, see page 104

Nouns

elephant	bus	sea
mountain	school	dog
window	drainpipe	tree
house	ant	road

Special words (1)

water	camouflage	temperature
burrow	forecast	strength
blowing	egg	attack
zoo	rainbow	scent
misty	clouds	kill
drops	coat	winter

SPEAKING AND
LISTENING

Special words (2)

nocturnal	satellite	hunt
sunshine	mammal	ice
cool	fast	biting
stripes	barometer	snow
teeth	puddles	timid
lightning	food	hurricane

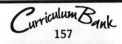
SPEAKING AND
LISTENING

INFORMATION TECHNOLOGY WITHIN SPEAKING AND LISTENING

Main IT focus

The information technology activities in this book can be used to develop and assess children's IT capability as outlined in the national curricula.

The main emphasis for the development of information technology skills within the activities is on communicating information specifically through the use of word processing.

Word processing

Although links between speaking and listening skills and IT may at first appear to be tenuous, there are many ways of using IT within the activities in this book. Many of the display ideas contain suggestions for scribing or simple writing activities; these can be carried out at the computer using a word processor or simple desktop publishing package. However, teachers will need to ensure that use of the computer does not detract from the main purpose of the activity and its emphasis on the development of speaking and listening skills.

Children should already have a basic knowledge of the keyboard and should be given opportunities to develop some of the more sophisticated aspects of using a word processor or desktop publishing package. These should include learning how to:

▲ use more than a single finger/hand when typing, particularly as children become more proficient and know the location of letters on the keyboard;

▲ separate and join text using the return and delete keys;

▲ move the cursor to a mistake and correct it without deleting all the text back to the mistake;

▲ scroll around the document using the mouse or cursor keys;

▲ select an appropriate font from a menu;

▲ change the size and/or colour of a font;

▲ underline a word or line;

▲ alter the style of a word or sentence, for example by using italics or bold;

▲ centre text using the centre command;

▲ use the tab key to create columns;

▲ right align, left align and fully justify text;

▲ save a document on disk and then retrieve it;

▲ print completed work;

▲ use a spelling checker to check work;

▲ add a picture, positioning and resizing it.

In addition, higher order skills include the ability to:

▲ alter the ruler to change margins and set tab keys;

▲ add page numbers;

▲ set up a master page to create a consistent layout throughout a document;

▲ set up a text style to use within a document.

Some children will take a long time to enter text at the keyboard so it is important to ensure that the word-processing tasks are kept short. It is important for teachers, or other adults who have relevant computer knowledge, to be available to intervene as children are working to teach them new skills appropriate to the tasks being undertaken.

Working at the computer from the outset of an IT activity is preferable to writing out work in longhand first and using the word processor solely to make a 'fair copy' for display purposes. However, it may be appropriate for children to make their first draft at the keyboard, save it, print it out and then redraft it away from the keyboard in order to give another child the opportunity to use the computer. They can then return later on to make any changes that they have decided upon and format the final copy for printing.

Multimedia authoring software

This software is a relatively recent addition for most schools but is proving to be a very versatile and powerful medium. It combines many of the features of a word processor or desktop publishing package but its main difference is that the different pages of a child's work can be linked together in an interactive sequence. Depending on the way that the links are created, children can move to different parts of the presentation by simply clicking with a mouse on a symbol, word or picture. Such presentations usually begin with a title page which allow the user to move to different chapters in a story, or sections of a presentation.

The other important feature is the software's ability to handle a range of different information including text, pictures from art and drawing packages, digitised pictures from scanned images, ion cameras and video cameras, sounds from audio CDs or sound samples. This enables children to record their own voices through a microphone which is linked to the computer. The recorded passages can be edited and then included within the overall presentation. It is also possible to include moving pictures taken from a CD-ROM or captured using a video camera. Some of these latter areas require specialised equipment but the mixing of text, pictures and simple recorded sounds can be undertaken with the minimal amount of equipment.

Work with authoring packages is best undertaken as a part of a longer project, with children working in groups. A class presentation can be split among several groups with each one preparing the text and pictures for their section and deciding how the pages are to be laid out and linked. Children will need support when they first start to put their ideas into the computer. They will need to know how to create frames, alter text styles, add colours, import graphics and sound files from other disks and make the links between pages. A class structure can be set up in advance by the teacher which gives a starting point for group work. It is advisable for the teacher to spend some time with the software before embarking on a project with children.

The grids on this page relate the activities in this book to specific areas of IT and to relevant software resources. Activities are referenced by page number, and bold page numbers indicate activities which have expanded IT content. The software listed is a selection of programs generally available to primary schools, and is not intended as a recommended list.

AREA OF IT	SOFTWARE	ACTIVITIES (PAGE NOS.)					
		CHAPTER 1	CHAPTER 2	CHAPTER 3	CHAPTER 4	CHAPTER 5	CHAPTER 6
Communicating information	Word processor	17, 19, 20, 24	**32**, 34, 40	46, 54, 58, 61	**65**, 68, 69, 75, 78, 79	**86**, 88, 91, 92	**100**
Communicating information	DTP	20	33, 34	46	**65, 76**		
Communicating information	Art package				79		
Communicating information	Drawing package		33	**60**	79		
Communicating information	Multimedia	24	34	47, **49**, **56**	69, **74**, 76	85, 87	
Communicating information	Framework	18					
Information handling	CD-ROM	16		60			
Information handling	Branching database			**59**			
Information handling	Database				67		
Control	Roamer		37				

SOFTWARE TYPE	BBC/MASTER	RISCOS	NIMBUS/186	WINDOWS	MACINTOSH
Word processor	Folio Pendown	Pendown Desk Top Folio	All Write Write On Caxton Press	Word Kid Works 2 Creative Writer	Kid Works 2 EasyWorks Creative Writer
DTP	Front Page Extra Typesetter	Desk Top Folio 1st Page Pendown DTP	Front Page Extra NewSPAper	Creative Writer NewSPAper Publisher	Creative Writer
Art package		Ist Paint Kid Pix Splash		Colour Magic Kid Pix 2	Kid Pix 2
Drawing package		Draw Picture IT			
Authoring		Hyperstudio Rainbow Portfolio		Hyperstudio MM Box	Hyperstudio
Branching database	Branch	ReTreeval Tree	Branch	Tree	
Database	Our Facts Grass Pigeonhole	DataSweet Find IT Junior Pinpoint	Our Facts Datashow	Sparks ClarisWorks Junior Pinpoint	ClarisWorks EasyWorks

SPEAKING AND LISTENING

	MATHS	SCIENCE	HISTORY	GEOGRAPHY	D & T	IT	ART	MUSIC	RE	PE
INFORMATION HANDLING		Summarising important information. Researching information for a talk. Researching information on a specific topic. Researching essential information for a zoo notice.	Summarising important information. Researching information for a talk.	Summarising important information. Researching information for a talk. Following given directions on a map. Researching information on a specific topic.		Use of word processor for planning and revising work and for text manipulation.		Researching information on a specific topic. Comparing and describing contrasting pieces of music.	Researching information for a talk.	Researching information on a specific topic. Providing essential information on how to play a game or sport.
EXPLAINING AND UNDERSTANDING	Finding the area of an irregular shape. Preparing a talk on a mathematical instrument.	Presenting a talk on a technology project. Adopting the persona of another character.	Adopting the persona of another character.	Giving directions to a specific destination. Following directions on a map.		Instructing others on how to play a computer game. Use of word processor for planning and revising work and for text manipulation.	Giving a verbal description of a picture.		Adopting the persona of another character.	
REASONING AND SPECULATING		Using deductive skills to recognise common dangers related to the home. Adopting the persona of an animal. Researching the design features of a garden for a visually impaired person. Discussing solutions to local and global problems.		Discussing solutions to local and global problems.	Researching the design features of a garden for a visually impaired person.	Use of word processor for planning and revising work and for text manipulation.	Building up a complete picture using small sections. Looking at appropriate colours for emotion words. Discussing favourite pictures.		Exploring moral dilemmas.	
OPINION AND PERSUASION		Assuming the persona of an animal. Exploring environmental issues.	Preserving items for future generations.	Exploring environmental issues.		As above.		Discussing favourite pieces of music.	Exploring moral dilemmas. Examining feelings.	
STORYTELLING AND PERFORMANCE		Adopting an alternative persona.	Adopting an alternative persona.	Adopting an alternative persona.		As above.				Adopting an alternative persona.
EXTENDING VOCABULARY		Brainstorming subject-specific vocabulary.		Brainstorming subject-specific vocabulary.		As above.				

SPEAKING AND LISTENING